Andrew Lucas (R189089)
(1919–1980)
'His Life – My Father'

There are not that many books about the 'real'
heroes of WW2, and those such as Andrew Lucas
deserve to be mentioned and remembered.

This real life story deals with the life of an
ordinary young man who became extraordinary
by the fact that he was unassuming
in his life and by what he achieved.

To cross the Atlantic the number of times
that he did took tremendous courage,
to be abandoned as a baby and survive takes
tremendous courage. This is a book about courage,
perseverance and humility.

Contents

Introduction

Andrew Lucas was born in 1919 in Hamilton, Lanarkshire. He was the second baby son of triplets born to Andrew and Elizabeth Lucas. Within 12 days two of the boys, Charles and James died. Andrew was the only surviving triplet.

Sometime between the ages of four and five years of age, Andrew was taken to Derry, Northern Ireland, to be raised by his two spinster aunts while the rest of his family immigrated to the USA.

His upbringing in Derry was harsh and cruel. He was badly treated by the Christian Brothers at school and by his aunts at home. At 14 years of age, Andrew stole 10 shillings from his aunt's purse and ran away to sea. He joined the Merchant Navy by pretending he was 16 years of age. His first job was as a Mess Boy.

When his ship docked in Glasgow in 1938, Andrew found some of his cousins. One of them took him to meet some other relatives, the Gibson family – one of whom, Mary (a third cousin) eventually became his wife.

The following year, when Andrew was 20 years of age, the Second World War began. Just two weeks before Britain officially declared war on Germany, Andrew's ship had been berthed in Hamburg.

During the war Andrew crossed on the Atlantic Convoy somewhere between 10 and 15 times. He was torpedoed on one ship and bombed from the air on another. He survived both.

Some of his family were not so fortunate. Four lost their lives in the Clydebank Blitz in 1941, with only two managing to survive.

In 1942, Andrew married Mary Frances Gibson. She was 19 years old, he was 22. In many respects, it was a 'marriage of convenience', as Mary would have been called up to the war effort if they had not married then.

On the 3rd of January 1944, while his ship was docked in Halifax, Nova Scotia, Canada, Andrew decided to jump ship and try to find his family who had settled in Chicago. He had made prior contact with them, so knew where to find them – but getting there did not prove to be easy. Andrew was classified as a 'deserter' and the Royal Canadian Mounted Police (RCMP) and the US authorities were looking for him.

After seven emotional and exhausting days Andrew returned to Halifax where he was arrested. Eventually he was exonerated and re-joined the war effort, but he never saw his parents again. His mother died in 1946 and his father lived till he was 90.

After the war Andrew – the father of six children – continued in the Merchant Navy, retiring on medical grounds in 1972. –Andrew Lucas died peacefully in February 1980. He qualified for seven medals for his contribution to the war effort, but did not collect or apply for them. His son, Thomas, is now the proud owner of five of them.

No.	Name and Surname	When and Where Died	Sex	Age	Name, Surname & Rank or Profession of Father; Name and Maiden Surname of Mother	Cause of Death, Duration of Disease, and Medical Attendant by whom certified	Signature & Qualification of Informant, and Residence, if out of the House in which the Death occurred	When and Where Registered, and Signature of Registrar
509	James Lucas (Single)	1919, December Ninth, 1h.50m. a.m. 5 Guthrie Street HAMILTON	M	10 Days	Andrew Lucas Coal Miner Elizabeth Lucas M.S. McClellan	Birth debility Illness of Life 2 Days As certified by John A. Thomson M.B. Ch.A.	Andrew Lucas Father	1919, December 16th At HAMILTON Marion Thomson Registrar
510	Charles Lucas (Single)	1919, December Eleventh 8h.15m. a.m. 5 Guthrie Miln C HAMILTON	M	12 Days	Andrew Lucas Coal Miner Elizabeth Lucas M.S. McClellan	Birth debility As certified by John A. Thomson M.B. Ch.A.	Andrew Lucas Father	1919, December 12th At HAMILTON Marion Thomson Registrar

EXTRACT OF AN ENTRY IN A REGISTER OF **BIRTHS**, kept in the undermentioned PARISH or DISTRICT, in terms of 17° & 18° VICTORIAE, Cap. 80, §§ 56 & 58.

(1) Name and Surname.	(2) When and Where Born.	(3) Sex.	(4) Name, Surname, and Rank or Profession of Father. Name, and Maiden Surname of Mother. Date and Place of Marriage.	(5) Signature and Qualification of Informant, and Residence, if out of the House in which the Birth occurred.	(6) When and Where Registered, and Signature of Registrar.
new —ucas	1919 November Twenty ninth 3h. 40m am 5 Guthrie Street HAMILTON	m	Andrew Lucas Coal miner Elizabeth Lucas m.s. McCallum 1915 October 22nd HAMILTON	Signed Andrew Lucas Father Baptised 6 Mr. J. T. Harkness Sahara Mината a/Carson 8th Feb 1920	1919 December 8' at HAMILTON Signed James Frame Registrar

EXTRACTED from the REGISTER BOOK OF BIRTHS, for the DISTRICT of HAMILTON
COUNTY of LANARK this 30' day of January 1920.

James Frame, Assistant Registrar

191_. BIRTHS in the DISTRICT of HAMILTON   in the COUNTY of LANARK

No.	Name and Surname.	When and Where Born.	Sex.	Name, Surname, & Rank or Profession of Father. Name, and Maiden Surname of Mother. Date and Place of Marriage.	Signature and Qualification of Informant, and Residence, if out of the House in which the Birth occurred.	When and Where Registered, and Signature of Registrar.
1321	James Lucas	1914 November Twentyninth 1h.40m. a.m. Gothic Street HAMILTON	M	Andrew Lucas Coal Miner Elizabeth Lucas M.S. McCallion 1915 October 27th HAMILTON	Andrew Lucas Father	1914 December 8th At HAMILTON Gavin Fraser Registrar.
1322	Andrew Lucas	1914 November Twentyninth 1h.40m. a.m. Gothic Street HAMILTON	M	Andrew Lucas Coal Miner Elizabeth Lucas M.S. McCallion 1915 October 22nd HAMILTON	Andrew Lucas Father	1914 November 8th At HAMILTON Gavin Fraser Registrar.
1323	Charles Lucas	1914 November Twentyninth 1h.40m. a.m. Gothic Street HAMILTON	M	Andrew Lucas Coal Miner Elizabeth Lucas M.S. McCallion 1915 October 22nd HAMILTON	Andrew Lucas Father	1914 December 8th At HAMILTON Gavin Fraser Registrar.

Quadruplet   Quadruplet   Quadruplet

CERTIFICATE OF BIRTH.

NATIONAL HEALTH INSURANCE ACT, 1924, and
UNEMPLOYMENT INSURANCE ACTS, 1920 to 1924.

Name and Surname	..	Andrew Lucas
When and where born	..	29ᵗʰ November 1914. 5. Authrie Street, Hamilton,
Name, Surname, &c., of Father	..	Andrew Lucas, Coal Miner
Name and Maiden Surname of Mother	..	Elizabeth Lucas, M. S. Mᶜ Lallin,
Date and place of Marge	..	1915. October 22ⁿᵈ Hamilton

I hereby certify that the above particulars are extracted by me from Entry No. 1322
in the Register Book of Bhs pertaining to the DISTRICT of HAMILTON in the
COUNTY of LANARK for the year 1914.

(Place) HAMILTON

(Date) 18ᵗʰ January 1935

Nat Lucas
Registrar.

Name and Surname.	When and Where Born.	Sex.	Name, Surname, and Rank or Profession of Father. Name, and Maiden Surname of Mother. Date and Place of Marriage	Signature and Qualification of Informant, and Residence, if out of the House in which the Birth occurred.	When and Where Registered, and Signature of Registrar.
Andrew Lucas	1919 November Twenty ninth 3h 40m am 5 Arthur Street HAMILTON	M	Andrew Lucas Coal miner & Elizabeth Lucas m.s. McCall 1915 October HAMILTON	(Signed) Andrew Lucas Father	1919 December 8 At HAMILTON (Signed) Graham Windols Registrar

Baptised 6
Mr J. T. Vankuer
at Carson 8th Feb 1920

EXTRACTED from the REGISTER BOOK of BIRTHS, for the DISTRICT of HAMILTON
...LANARK..., this 30 day of Jan... 1920. (Signed) ...ames Name Registrar.

1915 LUCAS, ANDREW - MCCALLION, ELIZABETH (Statutory Marriages 647/00 0233)

wright. Image was generated at 04 July 2007 20:31

(Para 117.)

(Page 117.)

1915   MARRIAGES in the DISTRICT of HAMILTON in the COUNTY of LANARK.

No.	When, Where, and How Married.	Signatures of Parties. Rank or Profession, whether Single or Widower, and Relationship (if any).	Age.	Usual Residence.	Name, Surname, and Rank or Profession of Father. Name, and Maiden Surname of Mother.	If a regular Marriage, Signatures of officiating Minister and Witnesses. If irregular, Date of Conviction, Decree of Declarator, or Sheriff's Warrant.	When & Where Registered, and Signature of Registrar.
233	1915. on the twenty second day of October at 14 Almada Street HAMILTON After Banns according to the forms of the Established Church of Scotland	(Signed) Andrew Lucas Coal hewer (Bachelor)	23	Almada Street HAMILTON	John Lucas pit coal hewer (Signed) Annie Lucas m. S. Jones	(Signed) Douglas M Bruce minister of Badgent Parish (Signed) Leonard Lucas Witness Mary Smith Witness	1915. October 23 at HAMILTON James Finnan Asst. Registrar
234	1915. on the twenty second day of October at Badgent Manse HAMILTON After Banns according to the forms of the Established Church of Scotland	(Signed) George Graham Saunders Pneumatic Shiftster (Bachelor) (Signed) Isabella Graham Housekeeper (Spinster)	40 44	John Street HAMILTON etc. orchard HAMILTON	John Saunders Blacksmith (Journeyman) Elizabeth Saunders m. S. Perceval (Both Deceased) John Graham Colliery Inspector Elizabeth Graham m. S. M Officer (Both Deceased)	(Signed) Douglas M Bruce minister of Badgent Parish (Signed) William Saunders Witness Catherine MacKenzie Witness	1915. October 23 at HAMILTON James Finnan Asst. Registrar

Foreword

Researching this book was initially a difficult and sometimes painful experience for me. It was hard to come to terms with the sad fact that I knew very little about my father. As a Merchant Seaman he would be away for many months at a time, which resulted in me and my siblings only getting glimpses of what he was like when he was at home. His story, however, is unusual and demands to be told.

The book is in part a cleansing of the soul. Although he was a major influence in my life and that of my brothers, Andrew and John, and my sisters, Mary, Ann and Agnes, he was denied the opportunity to be a part of our childhood and growing up. We missed out on his guidance and support.

This book is dedicated to his memory and, in some small way, an attempt to get to know who the 'real' Andrew Lucas was. No tears were shed in researching and writing this book – he would have been mortified if that was the case – but now and then I would get a lump in my throat.

This book is also in part dedicated to those Merchant Seamen who served so gallantly during the Second World War and who were so shabbily treated by the very people who depended on them for survival. Winston Churchill was correct when he said that the Battle of the Atlantic was the 'Battle FOR Britain'.

Chapter 1

The Early Years 1919-1922

Andrew Lucas was born on November 29, 1919 – the year after the 'Great War' had ended. His birth certificate identifies that he was born at 5 Guthrie Street, Hamilton at 3.40am – the second of triplets born to miner Andrew Lucas and his wife, Elizabeth. The couple already had two other children – John and Nan.

The two other triplets – also boys – were James and Charles. Unfortunately within two weeks they had both died. On the death certificate both babies were registered as having died from 'birth debility' (an abscess of the lip). James died on December 9th and Charles on December 11th.

Andrew and Elizabeth had married on October 22, 1915 at 17 Almada Street, Hamilton after posting banns according to the forms of the Established Church of Scotland. The marriage was presided over by the Reverend Douglas S Barnes, Minister of Cadzow Church. The newlyweds were both 23 years of age.

For the next few years the family lived at 5 Guthrie Street, Hamilton. But mining was difficult and dangerous for a young man with a growing family, and somewhere around 1922 Andrew and Elizabeth decided to emigrate to the USA and start a new life there. It appears that Andrew Senior travelled alone first, sailing on the Clyde-built SS Tuscania from Glasgow to New York on April 21, 1923.

Andrew, then 31 years of age, eventually arrived at Ellis Island, New York on May 1, 1923. In the official Ellis Island documentation, he was shown to have arrived with only 36 dollars in his possession and registered his intention to visit a friend – Thomas Morrison – in Philadelphia with the intention of seeing US citizenship.

Elizabeth and the two older children were to follow him to America but, as Andrew was the youngest, it was decided that he should be left behind. One of the main theories was that Andrew was too ill to travel such a long distance by boat. Another theory was that, as he was still so young, it would be better if he stayed behind to be sent for later. Whatever the real reason, Andrew was abandoned by his mother and father and taken to Northern Ireland to be raised by his two spinster aunts in Derry.

If this was intended to be a short, temporary measure, then it failed. The rest of the family were reunited and settled in Chicago, with three more children being born in the US – Thomas (1928), Marie (1929) and Elaine (1930).

Young Andrew, meanwhile, started his life over again in Derry. And it would be almost 20 years before he would set eyes on his mother and father again. It is believed that during the course of his life in Ireland, money was sent over for him to join his family in America. However no-one came across the Atlantic to get him.

Sadly there are no family records of his early childhood. What information that can be pieced together was that Andrew lived under a very strict regime with his aunts and attended the local Christian Brothers school, where corporal punishment was forever present.

Chapter 2

The Abandoned Years 1924-1933

In essence, not much is known about Andrew's early life in Pennyburn Avenue, Derry.

In later life, Andrew never really discussed this part of his life and he never passed on the reasons why he was abandoned by his parents. No doubt it could not have been an easy decision for his parents to make. But it is also hard to imagine just how traumatised this young boy must have felt when he realised that he was being left behind by his mother, father and older siblings.

It is clear that his two aunts were under the distinct impression that the youngster's stay with them would be relatively short, until his parents sent for him. Instead Andrew stayed with them for over 10 years and attended the local primary school in Pennyburn. Having never married nor had children of their own, his aunts had no idea how to raise children. The result was that he was unintentionally cruelly treated, with physical punishment the order of the day using either a rod or a leather belt.

From a very early age he was given chores to do around the house before he went to school. Often he would have to be up before 6am, and on his return from school further duties awaited him. There was no time in his life for childish play.

Atlantic Ports Passenger Lists, 1820-1873 and 1893-1959 record for Elizabeth Lucas

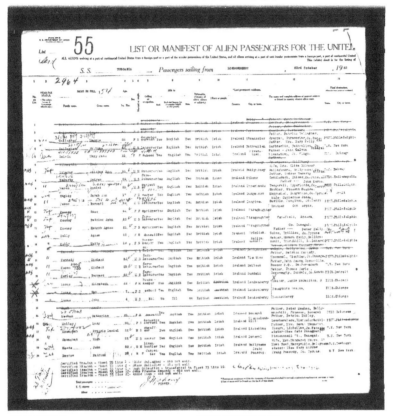

Record Index

Name: Elizabeth Lucas

Arrival Date: 1 Nov 1923

Age: 32 Years

Estimated birth year: abt 1891

Gender: Female

Ethnic Background: Irish

Port of Departure: Londonderry, Ireland

Ship Name: Tuscania

Port of Arrival: Portland, Maine

Source Information

Source Information:

Ancestry.com. *Atlantic Ports Passenger Lists, 1820-1873 and 1893-1959* [database online]. Provo, UT, USA: Ancestry.com Operations Inc, 2010.

Original data:

Atlantic Ports Passenger Lists, 1820-1873 and 1893-1959 record for Nan Lucas

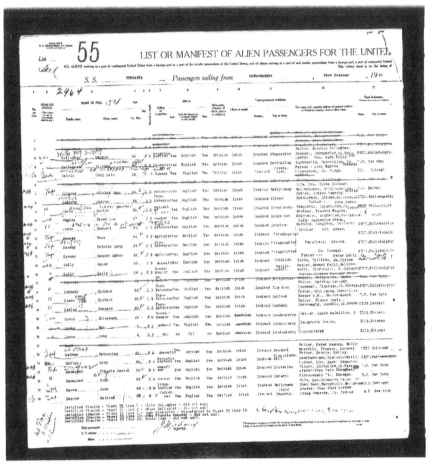

Record Index

Name: Nan Lucas

Arrival Date: 1 Nov 1923

Age: 7 Years

Estimated birth year: abt 1916

Gender: Female

Ethnic Background: Irish

Port of Departure: Londonderry, Ireland

Ship Name: Tuscania

Port of Arrival: Portland, Maine

Source Information

Record URL: http://search.ancestry.com/cgi-bin/sse.dll?
h=4128997&db=miscatlanticpl&indiv=try

Source Information: Ancestry.com. *Atlantic Ports Passenger Lists, 1820-1873 and 1893-1959* [database online]. Provo, UT, USA: Ancestry.com Operations Inc, 2010.
Original data:

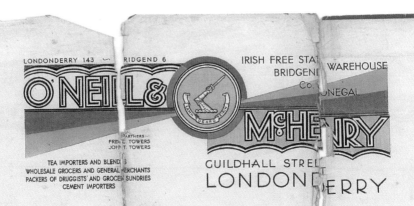

LONDONDERRY 143   RIDGEND 6

IRISH FREE STAT WAREHOUSE
BRIDGEND
Co. NEGAL

—PARTNERS—
FRED E. TOWERS
JOHN T. TOWERS

TEA IMPORTERS AND BLENDES
WHOLESALE GROCERS AND GENERAL MERCHANTS
PACKERS OF DRUGGISTS' AND GROCER SUNDRIES
CEMENT IMPORTERS

GUILDHALL STREL
LONDON ERRY

16TH
DECR.
193

WE HAVE KNOWN ANDREW LUCAS OF 4, PENNYBURN AVENUE, DERRY. FOR SOME TIME AND BELIEVE HIM TO BE A STEADY AND TRUSTWORTHY YOUNG MAN. HE HAS HAD A SOUND EDUCATION AND FOR SOME TIME PAST HAS BEEN EMPLOYED IN A CLERICAL CAPACITY DURING WHICH TIME HE GAVE EVERY SATISFACTION TO HIS EMPLOYER.

WE HAVE NO DOUBT HE WILL MAKE GOOD IN ANY CAPACITY FOR WHICH HE IS FOUND QUALIFIED.

PER PRO.

O'NEILL & MCHENRY,

PARTNER.

We do not know who his friends were or how he got on at school, but the economic depression was about to take its toll and money was very scarce. There is a strong rumour within the family that money was sent to Andrew's aunts to pay for his fare across the Atlantic. If true, the money never got to Andrew. There does appear to have been some form of sporadic communication between the child and his parents, but Andrew did not keep any of the letters sent to him.

By the time Andrew was 13 years of age, he had already suffered at the hands of his two maiden aunts and at school under the regime of the Christian Brothers, which was nothing short of brutal at times.

The Christian Brothers provided a 'Christian' education primarily for the sons of artisans and the poor, and a stern and strict religious culture permeated through the school. The corporal punishment administered by the Brothers was often appalling, and many children suffered terribly from physical and mental abuse.

As if being punished at school was not bad enough, Andrew also suffered at home. The slightest misdemeanour or mistake invariably involved some form of physical pain.

When he reached the age of 13, Andrew was sent out to work as a message boy and then a delivery boy for Messrs. O'Neil & McHenry. By 1933 he was employed by them in a clerical capacity. He was 14 years of age. A reference letter from O'Neils is attached.

This letter was to be Andrew's passport out of 4 Pennyburn Avenue, Derry.

Chapter 3
Running Away

For some time Andrew had been planning to run away from his aunts. On Friday, June 2nd, 1933, after finishing his work and then all his household chores, the teenager made up his mind to leave.

As he lay on his bed, Andrew began to put his plan into operation. He thought that his best plan was to escape to sea, as no-one would be able to follow him there.

He packed some clothes into a small case ready for his escape and approximately 6am on Saturday, June 3, gathered all his meagre belongings and crept out of his bedroom. He noticed that one of his aunts had left her purse on top of a cabinet, so he took 30 shillings. He quietly opened the front door and, closing it behind him, left 4 Pennyburn Avenue forever. He would never return.

It did not take him long to reach the dock area of Derry. Although it was a busy port, with several boats coming and going in and out of the harbour, Andrew was not sure about how to join a ship. The Seaman's Mission was nearby and Andrew reckoned that this would be a good place to start. On entering Andrew asked the duty manager if there were any ships looking for workers. The manager was unsure when Andrew claimed to be 16 years old (he was only 14) and asked for his National Insurance card. Andrew convincingly replied that he was waiting for it to arrive as he had just left school, so the manager agreed to ask around for any vacancies.

After a nervous wait for Andrew, the manager returned to say there was a ship leaving later that day and they were looking for a Mess Boy. Andrew wrote down the details, thanked the manager and set off to look for the ship. When he found it, he walked tentatively up the gangplank to report to the Captain.

The Captain, while friendly, was immediately wary of how young Andrew looked. But the teenager handed over his reference from O'Neil and McSherry, merchants who were well known in Derry.

Despite his youthful appearance, Andrew had a hardened maturity about him and a steely determination, so the Captain decided that he would take him on as a Mess Boy.

Calling over one of the seamen, the Captain instructed him to take Andrew down to the kitchen to report to the chef. The ship was a sea-going tanker with a large crew.

Andrew was introduced to the chef then taken to his bunk and told to put his belongings in a locker, before returning to the kitchen to be given a list of his duties. As a Mess Boy he would be a gofer and a skivvy to the Captain, his officers and the rest of the crew. Little did he know what he was letting himself in for!

Back in Pennyburn Avenue, the two aunts were wakening up to find that Andrew had gone, but were oblivious to the fact that he had run away. They thought he had just gone out to work as normal and it wasn't until late in the evening that they became concerned. By the time they notified the police, Andrew was long gone.

According to the police, Andrew would become just another 'missing person'. It would be quite some time before they would find out that he was alive and well, but their immediate problem was how to tell his parents in the United States. So they decided not to.

On board the ship, Andrew was busy in the kitchen. He was taught how to set the table for Captain and his officers, and he helped with serving the food and cleaning up. By the time he had finished all that he was asked to do, Andrew lay down on his bunk and fell fast asleep. The engines roared into life and the ship began to leave Derry harbour. By midnight the ship was far out to sea, and a new chapter in the life of Andrew Lucas was about to begin.

His two aunts never recovered from Andrew running away. Eventually his parents were informed. The police made an attempt at searching for him, but eventually classified his as a missing person. Although he was 14 years of age, there were no photos of him to hand around and his friends and neighbours had no idea where he would have gone. It was not until he returned to the UK that Andrew applied for his NI card and passport.

Over the next four or five years Andrew 'grew up' and became a hardened sailor. He rose from Mess Boy to Sailor – a case of sink or swim. That meant he had to look after himself in a physical sense too. Life at sea was no picnic; in reality it was often harsh and brutal.

Clan Mactaggart

British Steam merchant

Photo courtesy of State Library of New South Wales

Name	Clan Mactaggart
Type:	Steam merchant
Tonnage	7,622 tons
Completed	1920 - Ayrshire Dockyard Co Ltd, Irvine
Owner	The Clan Line Steamers Ltd (Cayzer, Irvine & Co Ltd), London
Homeport	Glasgow
Date of attack	16 Nov 1942 **Nationality:** 🇬🇧 British

Fate	Sunk by U-92 (Adolf Oelrich)
Position	36.08N, 07.23W - Grid CG 9457
Complement	172 (3 dead and 169 survivors).
Convoy	MKS-1X
Route	Gibraltar (15 Nov) - Clyde
Cargo	Ballast
History	Completed in November 1920
Notes on loss	At 05.49 hours on 16 Nov, 1942, the **Clan Mactaggart** (Master Joseph Henry Crellin) in convoy MKS-1X was torpedoed and sunk by U-92 50 miles southwest of Cadiz. Two crew members and one naval personnel were lost. The master, 97 crew members, 17 gunners and 54 naval personnel were picked up by **HMS Coreopsis (K 32)** (LtCdr A.H. Davies, RNVR). The survivors were distributed by the corvette to **HMS Landguard (Y 56)** (LtCdr T.S.L. Fox-Pitt, RN) and **HMS Lulworth (Y 60)** (LtCdr C. Gwinner, DSO, RN) and landed at Londonderry. 34 Lascars on **HMS Lulworth** were later transferred to the Havildar sailing in the same convoy.

There are no official records of Andrew's early life at sea until 1938. It was then, when he was genuinely 18 years old and had served in the Merchant Navy for several years, that he was recognised as a Seaman and given a unique reference number. This number would continue with him all though his sea career – R1890897.

The first ship on which Andrew was officially mentioned was the Alcora, a steamship of some 562 tonnage. Andrew is recorded in his official discharge book as a Messroom Boy, with the place of engagement as Glasgow on 3/3/1939 and discharge in Belfast on 18/7/1939. The Master of the ship, a Mr W. Reid, stamped Andrew's discharge book as being 'very good for ability' and 'very good for general conduct'.

On leaving the Alcora, Andrew joined the Clan Mactaggart – a cargo ship with a net tonnage of 4674 and registered in Glasgow.

During 1938 the Clan Mactaggart sailed from Glasgow to Liverpool, Port Natal, Beira, Calcutta, Table Bay, Buenos Aires, Balia Blanca, Cape Verde, Antwerp and back to Glasgow. After a short turnaround, she then sailed to Gibraltar, Port Said, Suez and then Aden, where Andrew and his fellow crew celebrated Christmas Day.

In January 1939 the Clan Mactaggart set sail for Madagascar, Calcutta, Chittagong, back to Madagascar, Tuti, Suez, Port Said, Gibraltar, and finally arrived in London on February 24. Shore leave was in short supply and, as Andrew did not have any relatives in London, he tended to stay on board or hung around the dock area.

On March 2nd, the Clan Mactaggart set sail for Antwerp then back to Liverpool on April 7. After another quick turnaround, she set sail again and arrived in Table Bay on May 2nd, Port Elizabeth on May 6th, East London on May 10th, Durban on May 12th, Mauritius on May 19th, London on June 4th, Visayan on June 11th, Aden on July 6th, Suez on July 11th, Port Said on July 12th, Gibraltar on July 18th, Avon on July 23rd, Lizard on July 31st, Dover on August 2nd and the German port of Hamburg on August 3rd.

Just one month after the Clan Mactaggart's brief visit to Hamburg, Britain declared war on Germany and the Second World War began.

This was one of the many lucky escapes which Andrew would have during this turbulent period. On August 10th Andrew and his crewmates arrived in Glasgow where they stayed until August 30th. Once again, a chance encounter was about to change his life.

Chapter 4
Arrival in Glasgow

By the time Andrew arrived in Glasgow for the first time, he had already been at sea for five years. He was 19 years of age. He had sorted out the issue of his disappearance with his aunts in Derry, and had established contact with his parents in Chicago. He had also been given the name and address of a cousin – Hughie Gallacher, who lived in Crail Street, Parkhead, Glasgow. Andrew had been in touch with Hughie and informed him that he would be coming to Glasgow that August.

When his ship docked on August 10th, it was not due to sail again for another two weeks so Andrew was given some shore leave. Two days later he headed out from the Broomielaw and made his way to Argyle Street where he found a tram which would take him to Parkhead Cross.

From there he was given directions to Crail Street, where Hughie and his wife, Martha, lived in a single-end tenement with an outside toilet on a half-landing. Having been given prior notice of Andrew's arrival, Hughie was waiting for him and the youngster was given a warm welcome by his cousin and Martha, spending several hours catching up on family affairs.

As the public houses in Glasgow closed every afternoon from 2pm to 5pm, Hughie could not take Andrew for a drink. At 5pm they ventured around the corner to O'Kane's public house on Westmuir Street where they sat and drank until closing time at 10pm, then returned to Hughie's house with a 'carry-out' bought in O'Kanes.

The following morning, still suffering from a massive hangover, Hughie suggested taking Andrew to visit some other relatives in the Shettleston area. In particular, he wanted to introduce him to the Gibson family at 146 Quarryknowe Street, which was only a 10 minute walk from Crail Street.

That afternoon the pair set off to visit the Gibson family – comprising the parents David and Mary, their sons David and Alphonsus, and daughters Mary Frances, Agnes, Sadie and Anne – who lived in a two bedroom house which boasted both an inside toilet and an inside coal bunker.

When they arrived, Mary Senior welcome them and made tea while the rest of the family were still at school or work. By early evening the rest of the family had returned and Andrew was introduced to them all.

At dinner, Andrew noticed young Mary, who was only about 17 at the time. After they had all eaten and washed up, the family settled down to play cards and listen to the crystal wireless set. The evening finished with a sing-song, with Andrew playing a selection of folk songs on his mouth organ. When Hughie and Andrew left at 11pm, Mrs Gibson insisted that Andrew come back to see them before his ship departed at the end of the month.

Andrew in fact visited the Gibsons on several occasions over the next few weeks, as his eye was drawn towards young Mary. And by the time his ship was due to leave, he was well and truly smitten by the young girl.

Although not much of a letter writer, Andrew and Mary began to write to each other. And every time his ship berthed in Glasgow, he headed straight for the Gibson home to see her. The young man loved going to this cheerful family home, and was extremely fond of Mary's mother. In some respects she became the mother that Andrew had never had.

The pair had a great relationship and enjoyed nothing more than the Sunday night ritual of playing cards and listening to the radio together. Invariably Andrew and Mrs Gibson would be cheating and the sound of laughter could be heard outside.

Chapter 5

The War Years 1939-1945
(a) At Sea, September – December 1939

Having narrowly escaped being in Germany at the outbreak of the Second World War when his ship was berthed in Hamburg, Andrew soon found himself catapulted into it.

Two days after Hitler invaded Poland on September 1, 1939, Britain and France declared war on Germany, and the then Prime Minister Neville Chamberlain appointed Winston Churchill as First Lord of the Admiralty.

By this time Andrew was on board the Clan MacTaggart which eventually arrived in Durban on October 10. During the next two months she travelled to Mauritius, Calcutta, Chittagong, Madagascar, Aden, Suez and Port Said, before arriving finally in Gibraltar on December 29.

Andrew was by now officially a sailor. As the war intensified, so the seas became more and more treacherous due to the silent warriors called submarines. Avoiding them was a hazardous occupation, but there was the added danger of being dive-bombed from above by enemy aircraft. These concerns were never far from the minds of all seamen.

(b) The War Years 1939-1945
1940

At the beginning of 1940 the Second World War was well underway, and the sea had become an important battleground. Merchant Navy convoys were now at the mercy of German submarines, aircraft and battleships.

The Clan Mactaggart left Gibraltar and arrived in London on January 7. From there she sailed to Glasgow, arriving on February 7, and was due to stay there for two or three weeks. This gave Andrew some time to go and see the Gibsons, especially Mary.

On March 23 the ship set sail again and arrived in Liverpool three days later. On March 31 she left the River Mersey heading for Gibraltar. From then until October that year the ship travelled to Port Said, Suez, Aden, Madagascar, Vizag, Ceylon, Lourenço Marques, Table Bay, Rio De Janeiro, Santos, Rosario, Buenos Aires, NV, Freetown and Liverpool, arriving there on October 9.

Two days later, while berthed at Liverpool, the Clan Mactaggart was hit by bombs in a night-time raid by German aircraft. Two other steam ships – the Clan Cumming and Highland Chieftain – and a tanker, Virgilia, were also damaged in the attack.

The Clan Mactaggart travelled to Glasgow nine days later for repairs, and remained there for almost one month.

This gave Andrew some more time to visit Mary and her family. The pressure and stress of the war made it difficult to make any future plans, and every time Andrew left to go to see Mary he

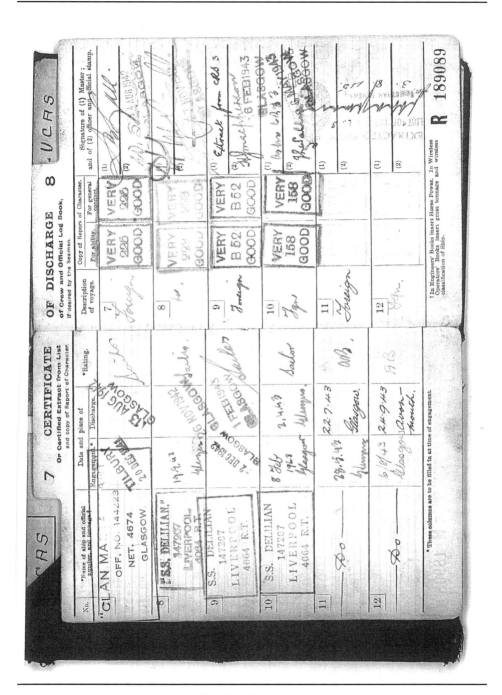

CERTIFICATE OF DISCHARGE

Or Certified Extract from List and copy of Report of Character

of Crew and Official Log Book, if desired by the Seaman.

No.	Name of ship and official number, and tonnage.†	Date and place of Engagement*	Discharge.	*Rating.	Description of voyage.	Copy of Report of Character. For ability.	For general conduct.	Signature of (1) Master; and of (2) officer and official stamp.
13	Empire Lousley 169023 Sunderland N.T. 4954.	1.10.43 Glasgow	20.10.43 Glasgow	A/B	13 Sgn.	VE		(1) contracted from Engr. (2) John Jerman per Registrar General 8.8.43 H.O
14 16	SAMGLORY	21.3.44 Glasgow	12.4.45 Barra	A/B	14/16 Sgn.	VERY B.52 GOOD	VERY B.52 GOOD	(1) GRS 2 (2) GLASGOW 25 JUL 1945
15 14	Clan Colquhoun 142741 Glasgow N.T. 4888.	24.12.43 Glasgow	Voyage not completed	A.B	15/14 Foreign	Voyage not Completed		(1) per Registrar General 3.8.45 H.O
16 17	DORELIAN 147212	8.6.45 Glasgow	13.7.45 Sgow	A.B	16/17 99—	VERY B.52 GOOD	VERY B.52 GOOD	(1) GRS 3 (2) GLASGOW
17 15	Bayano 141870 Glasgow N.T. 3735	3.2.44 Glasgow	26.2.44 Halifax Dock West	A.B	17/15 Foreign			(1) LIST OF CREW (2) John Jerman per Registrar General 3.8.45
18	Dorelian 147212 L'Pool	1.8.46 Glasgow Poplar	9.9.46	A.B	18 Sgn.	VERY B.53 GOOD	VERY B.53 GOOD	(1) LUCAS (2)

† In Engineers' Books insert Horse-Power. In Wireless Operators' Books insert gross tonnage and wireless classification of Ship.

* These columns are to be filled in at time of engagement.

R 189089

HOME | PHOTOS | VIDEOS | AIS | FORUM | NEWS | SUMMARY | CONTACT | WARFARE |
PHOTO INDEX | MOST POPULAR | NEW PHOTOS | CATEGORIES | PHOTO SEARCH | ADD PHOTO | MY PHOTOS |

CLAN COLQUHOUN

Photo Details

Photographer:	Rik [view profile]	Title:	CLAN COLQUHOUN	Added:	Aug 09, 2011
Captured:		IMO:	Unavailable	Hits:	513

Photo Category: General cargo ships built 1940 and before (Over 3000gt)

Description:
SS Clan Colquhoun (2) built 1918, ex-Gallic, 1933 purchased from White Star Line, renamed Clan Colquhoun, 1947 sold to Panama, renamed Ioannis Livanos, 7,912 tons

Vessel identification	Technical Data	AIS information
	Vessel type: -	AIS information: N/A

		Additional Information
Name:	N/A	
IMO:	N/A	Owner: -

Ship information by AtoZav ShipTrax and GrossTonnage.com. Report error in ship details

Delilian

British Steam merchant

Name	Delilian
Type:	Steam merchant
Tonnage	6,423 tons
Completed	1923 - D. & W. Henderson & Co Ltd, Glasgow
Owner	Donaldson Brothers Ltd, Glasgow
Homeport	Liverpool
Date of attack	7 Mar 1941 **Nationality:** British

Fate	Damaged by U-70 (Joachim Matz)
Position	60.28N, 13.38W - Grid AM 1244
Complement	68 (0 dead and 68 survivors).
Convoy	OB-293
Route	Glasgow - St. John, New Brunswick
Cargo	General cargo
History	Completed in April 1923 for F. Leyland & Co Ltd, Liverpool. 1934 sold to Charente SS Co Ltd (T. & J. Harrison) Liverpool. 1936 transferred to Donaldson Brothers Ltd, Glasgow.

At 01.16 hours on 24 Feb, 1943, U-653 (Feiler) fired a stern torpedo at the convoy ON-166 in 46°02N/39°20W. The torpedo missed the intended target but detonated near the **Delilian** without damaging her.

Post-war:
Broken up at Port Glasgow in February 1954.

Notes on event	On 7 Mar, 1941, U-70 attacked the convoy OB-293 southeast of Iceland, but was lost after a second attack at 07.25 hours. The survivors claimed that they had hit three ships in the first attack at 04.45 hours and another in the second. In fact they had hit Athelbeach and **Delilian** in station #71 and #61 during the first attack and Mijdrecht during the second.

At about 04.50 hours, the **Delilian** was hit on the starboard side by one torpedo and her crew abandoned ship. When **Mijdrecht** approached one of her lifeboats about 90 minutes later, she was herself damaged by a torpedo from the same U-boat. Escorts later brought the crew back to **Delilian** which turned back and arrived at Kames Bay on 10 March. She was repaired at Glasgow and returned to service in May 1941.

worried that he might never return. Having just survived one bombing raid, there was always the worry that he might not be so lucky next time.

On returning to his ship, Andrew and the Clan Mactaggart sailed from the tail of the Bank on a damp November day down to Liverpool to be loaded with cargo for the next voyage to Table Bay. The ship arrived there on December 20 and travelled on to dock in Durban on Christmas Eve, 1940.

(c) The Second World War 1941

Having survived the first full year of war and a bombing attack on his ship, Andrew saw the start of 1941 still serving on the Clan Mactaggart. By now he was a fully fledged sailor.

On January 2nd, she sailed from Durban, South Africa to Trincomalee, arriving there on the 26th. She stayed there for three days and then moved on to Madagascar, before her course took her to Chittagong & Vizag, berthing there on Valentine's Day. She made the return back to Durban and Table Bay, then onto Freetown, South Africa before making the perilous journey across the Atlantic and home to Glasgow on March 29th. She managed to escape enemy submarines and aircraft bombers.

By the beginning of May 1941 Andrew was still with the Clan Mactaggart. She left the Clyde on the 18th, docking in Liverpool on the 19th, then left nine days later for Table Bay. She arrived there safely on May 28, again successfully avoiding German aircraft, submarines and battleships. Having docked in Table Bay on June 28, she then moved to East London, then Durban.

After safely navigating the perilous South Atlantic and the enemy warships, the Clan Mactaggart set sail for Ceylon on July 12 and arrived there on 28/7/1941. After unloading her cargo, the next stop was Madras on the August 8, then Chittagong on August 19. Once the cargo was unloaded, the Clan Mactaggart sailed back to Madras, then onto Durban, Table Bay and finally Freetown on October 23.

Once all her Far Eastern journeys were over, the Clan Mactaggart had to renegotiate the perilous South Atlantic to sail back to Britain once more, before safely docking at Tilbury Docks on December 19. This was to be Andrew's last voyage with the ship. Once again, it proved to be a lucky move as the following year – on November 16, 1942 – the Clan Mactaggart was torpedoed by a German U-boat and sank 100 miles west of Gibraltar on its voyage to Liverpool. Three men were killed.

(d) The War Years 1939 – 1945: The Clydebank Blitz, 1941

While Andrew and his fellow crew were dodging enemy aircraft and submarines on the other side of the world, his friends and family back in Scotland were going through difficult times of their own.

Over two nights on the 13th and 14th of March 1941, the German Luftwaffe carried out a

Clydebank Blitz
13/14 March 1941

'His Life – My Father'

This map, compiled and designed by the artist in 1983, is included as part of the artist's research for the paintings titled "Map" It shows the town of Clydebank as it was in 1941. It contains detailed information of the damage caused by the raids of 13th and 14th March and illustrates the devastating accuracy and concentration of the attack.

The circles that surround the red bomb hits indicate the explosive category of individual bombs and are drawn at 'severe blast damage diameter'. The smaller rings indicate 50kg bombs...and progressively...250 kg bombs....500kg bombs. The largest rings...' Parachute Mines'... weighing almost 1 metric ton, had a severe blast damage radius of around half of one mile and are shown on the map at 'half damage scale' for clarity.

Thousands of incendiaries fell in the target area. Incendiary damage is shown by yellow spots. These do not indicate individual incendiaries but buildings destroyed by incendiary devices. Buildings are colour coded in a range from pink, totally destroyed - to black. minor damage.

In total only 7 houses out of a stock of 12,000 remained undamaged. Approximately 4,000 destroyed, 4,500 severely damaged and 3,500 in the serious to minor damage category.

In total 400+ high explosive bombs and mines fell in an area of less than two square miles, not including the 96 high explosive bombs that fell on the primary target...the oil tanks at Dalnottar to the north west of the town, or the 190 bombs that fell in the boundaries of the nearby villages of Duntocher, Hardgate, Bowling and Old Kilpatrick. 132 bombs fell in the Kilpatrick hills, aimed at decoy fires west of Cochno.

The greatest damage was caused by incendiaries. On the first night of the raid 1,630 containers of incendiary bombs (weighing between 70kg and 250kg) were dropped by the Luftwaffe, a total of 105,300 1kg bombs. On the second night 782 containers were dropped

According to German sources a total of 503 metric tons of high explosive bombs and 2,412 containers of incendiaries were dropped on Clydeside on the 13th and 14th March 1941. A total of 439 aircraft took part in the raids.

brutal and sustained attack on the town of Clydebank. Due to its geographical and industrial profile, Clydebank was a prime target. On that first night the Germans dropped 1,630 1kg incendiary bombs, but that was the precursor to the main bombing force which was to follow. Hardly a street in Clydebank survived without a casualty, with Second Avenue experiencing the highest number of casualties – 80.

On the second night, while Clydebank was still burning, the Luftwaffe returned to finish their task. When the last bomb exploded (see attached photos/maps) Clydebank had suffered a severe loss of housing. 4,500 houses were completely destroyed, 3,500 were severely damaged and only seven out of a stock of 12,000 remained intact.

Industrial targets received direct hits or incendiary damage. Beardmore, The Royal Ordnance Factory, John Brown's shipyard, Arnott Young, Rothesay Dock, D7J Tullis and the Singer factory were all hit. The massive Singer timber yard was destroyed, as was the oil storage depot at Dalnottar, which contained 11 huge tanks. When all the bomb sites were cleared some 96 bomb craters were counted.

However it was the human cost that was the most devastating. When the bombing eventually stopped on the 14th March, some 528 people had died, over 617 had been seriously injured, and many hundreds suffered cuts. The town was subsequently evacuated, with around 48,000 refugees sent to places far away.

Andrew Lucas lost some of his family in the Clydebank Blitz. Only two members of the Gallagher family who resided in John Knox Street, survived. They were Andrew's cousins. Andrew was given the sad news by the Gibsons when he docked in Glasgow. Although he did not know those cousins too well, Andrew still felt the loss greatly.

(e) August 1942
Marriage of Convenience

In 1942, Andrew was engaged in war service on board the SS Delilian – a boat which had survived a torpedo attack in March the previous year and been repaired back in Glasgow. But Andrew had more important things on his mind than attacks by the enemy.

On 24th August that year, at 9am, Andrew Lucas, Able-Bodied Seaman in the Merchant Navy, aged 22, of no fixed abode, married Mary Frances Gibson, a tailor's presser, aged 19, of 146 Quarryknowe Street, Shettleston, Glasgow.

The ceremony was carried out by Fr. James Kearney in St. Mark's RC church. The best man was Mr. John Murphy, of 322 Gallowgate, Parkhead, and the bridesmaid was Agnes Gibson, sister of Mary Frances Gibson.

There was no honeymoon for the young couple, as war was still raging. There was a Wedding Breakfast of sorts but, as there had been rationing since 1941, there was sadly no wedding cake. The young couple went back to 146 Quarryknowe Street for their wedding breakfast, which was attended by all the Gibson family and a few friends and neighbours.

Gallagher, Delia, age 15. 13th March 1941, at 10 Pattison Street.

Gallagher, Margaret Teresa Donaghue, age 30; of 8 East Barns Street. 13th March 1941, at 2
Napier Street.

Gallagher, Thomas, age 13; of 74 John Knox Street. Son of Thomas and Mary Gallagher. 13th
March 1941, at 2 Napier Street.

Galloway, Thomas Thomson, age 22; of 57 Whitecrook Street. Son of James Galloway, and of
Martha Thomson Galloway. 14th March 1941, at 57 Whitecrook Street.

(For Galloway, Martha see Glasgow List)*

Geddes (otherwise Thomson), William, age 15; of 57 Whitecrook Street. Son of Helen Wade
(formerly Geddes). 14th March 1941 , at 57 Whitecrook Street. (His Sister Jessie
Chalmers Wade was also killed in the same incident)

Gibson, John Young, age 54; of 6 Whin Street. Son of the late James and Margaret Neish
Gibson; husband of Mary Rae Gibson. 13th March 1941, at Whin Street.

Gillies, Annie, age 62; of 76 Seond Avenue. 13th March, at Second Avenue.

Gillies, Margaret McLaren, age 23; of 76 Second Avenue. Daughter of Annie Gillies. 13th
March 1941, at Second Avenue.

Given, Elizabeth, age 30; of 57 Whitecrook Street. Daughter of Mr. and Mrs. W.J. Reid, of
432 Dumbarton Road, Dalmuir; wife of WilliamGiven. 14th March 1941, at 57
Whitecrook Street.

Although Andrew had little contact with his family in the USA, he did receive a telegram from them in October that year wishing him and Mary all the 'best of happiness' (see enclosed telegram). In addition to the austere circumstances, Andrew and Mary also had the problem of having no place to live. But they were helped out by Mary's aunt, Martha Gallacher. She gave them a room in 20 Thornhill Street, Parkhead, which later became their permanent home.

Although the newlyweds were clearly a couple in love, it should be noted that the marriage itself was also a 'marriage of convenience'. When Andrew had arrived in Glasgow around 1939 he had been introduced to Mary through a cousin of the Gibson family. As he was a seaman, he did not enjoy many days ashore, especially when the Second World War started, so it would have been difficult for any relationship to flourish.

In addition Mary Frances would only have been 16 when she was first introduced to Andrew. To be married at the age of 19 years, even in 1942, was considered quite young.

However the main reason for their decision to marry at that time was that Mary Frances Gibson was likely to be called up for National Service. Parliament had passed the National Service Act in 1941, thereby conscripting young men and women to assist in the war effort. As married women were exempt, Andrew and Mary's marriage of 'convenience' served its purpose. The fact that they were married for over 30 years, however, testifies that they made the right decision.

Sadly it was not long before Andrew had to leave his young bride and rejoin the SS Delilian to continue his part in the war effort. The departure must have been heartbreaking for Andrew, and Mary could have been forgiven for wondering if she would ever see her husband again. This scenario would be repeated many times during the Second World War, and every time it happened must have been harder for Mary Frances to accept.

K

CT OF AN ENTRY IN A REGISTER OF **MARRIAGES**, kept in the undermentioned PARISH or DISTRICT, in terms of 17° & 18° VICTORIÆ, Cap. 80, §§ 56 & 58.

(1) When, Where, and How Married.	(2) Names (in full) of Parties, with Signatures—Rank or Profession, and whether Bachelor, Spinster, Widower, Widow, or Divorced.	(3) Age.	(4) Usual Residence.	(5) Name, Surname, and Rank or Profession of Father. Name, and Maiden Surname of Mother.	(6) If a Regular Marriage, Signatures and Designation of Officiating Minister or Registrar, and Signatures and Addresses of Witnesses. If an Irregular Marriage, Date or Decree of Declarator, or of Sheriff's Warrant.	(7) When and Where Registered, and Signature of Registrar.
1942 Twenty-fourth AUGUST St. Mark's Church GLASGOW	Andrew Lucas (Signature) Andrew Lucas (Merchant Navy) (Bachelor)	24	Now engaged in war service	Andrew Lucas Carl Miner Elizabeth Lucas M/s McCallion	(Signd) James Kearney Catholic Clergyman St. Mark's Carntyne Glasgow.	1942 AUGUST AT GLASG
	Mary Frances Gibson (Signature) Mary H. Gibson Tailor's Presser (Spinster)	19	146 Quarryknowe Street, Glasgow	David Gibson Housepainter (First Aid Worker) Civil Defence) Mary Frances Gibson M/s Gallagher	(Signd) John Murphy 339 Gallowgate Glasgow Witness Agnis Gibson 146 Quarryknowe Street Glasgow Witness	(Signed) A. M. Shea REGIST

EXTRACTED from the REGISTER BOOK of MARRIAGES for the DISTRICT of SHETTLESTON
GLASGOW , this 25 day of AUGUST 1942.

UBLICATION

g to the Forms of the Church

Am Shearer, Regis

ns of the 58th Section of the Act 17 & 18 Vict. c. 80, every Extract of an Entry in the Register kept by a Registrar under the provisions of the Registration of Births, Death (Scotland) Acts, duly authenticated and signed by the Registrar, is admissible as evidence in all parts of His Majesty's dominions without any other or further proof of such Entry. erson who falsifies any of the particulars on this Extract or makes use of such falsified Extract as true, knowing it to be false, is liable to prosecution.

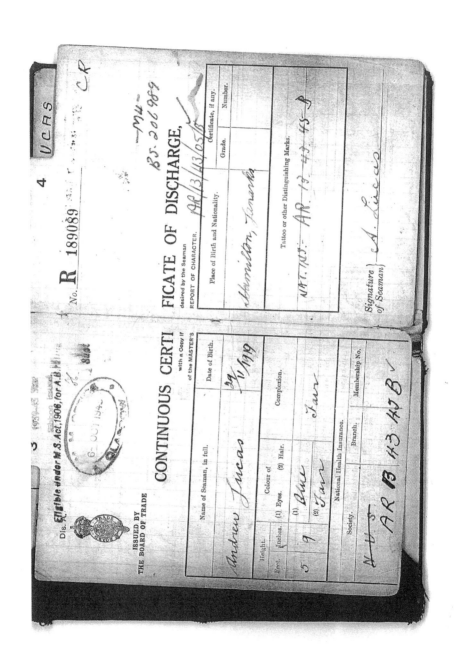

ARRIVALS POSTED IN BLACK,	SAILINGS AND	SPEAKINGS IN RED,	PARAGRAPHS IN BLUE.

SHIP'S NAME.	NET TONNAGE.	PORT OF REGISTRY.	CAPTAIN.
CLAN MACTAGGART	4674	Glasgow	

CLAN MACTAGGART

SHIP'S NAME.	NET TONNAGE.	PORT OF REGISTRY.
	4674	Glasgow

CAPTAIN.

ARRIVALS POSTED IN BLACK.	SAILINGS AND	SPEAKINGS IN RED,	PARAGRAPHS IN BLUE.

SHIP'S NAME.	NET TONNAGE.	PORT OF REGISTRY.	CAPTAIN
CLAN MACTAGGART	4674	GLASGOW	

ARRIVALS POSTED IN BLACK. | SAILINGS AND | SPEAKINGS IN RED. | PARAGRAPHS IN BLUE.

SHIP'S NAME. DELILIAN
NET TONNAGE. 4064
PORT OF REGISTRY. Liverpool
CAPTAIN.

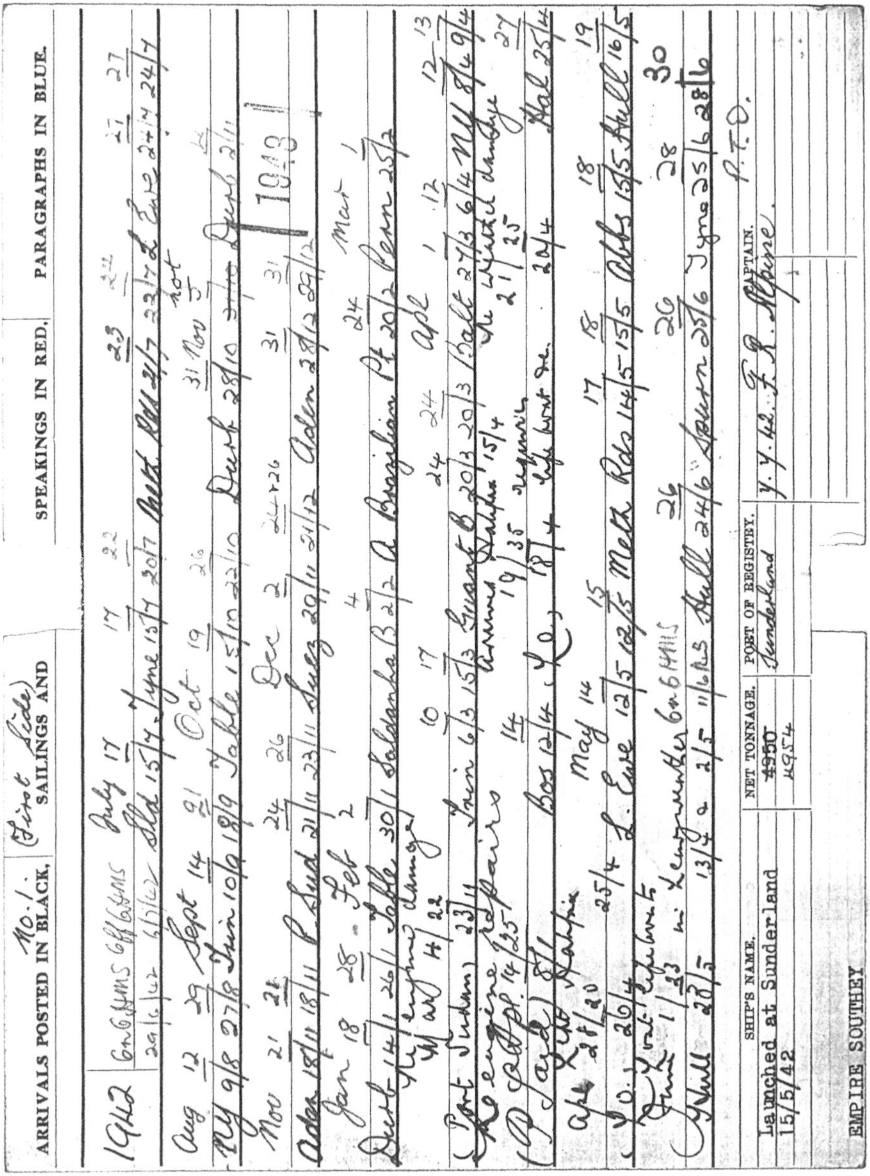
No. 1. (First Side)
ARRIVALS POSTED IN BLACK, SAILINGS AND SPEAKINGS IN RED, PARAGRAPHS IN BLUE.
1942
1943
SHIP'S NAME.
Launched at Sunderland
15/5/42
NET TONNAGE.
4950
4954
PORT OF REGISTRY.
Sunderland
CAPTAIN.
Y. Y. 42. F. R. Alpine.
P.T.O.
EMPIRE SOUTHEY

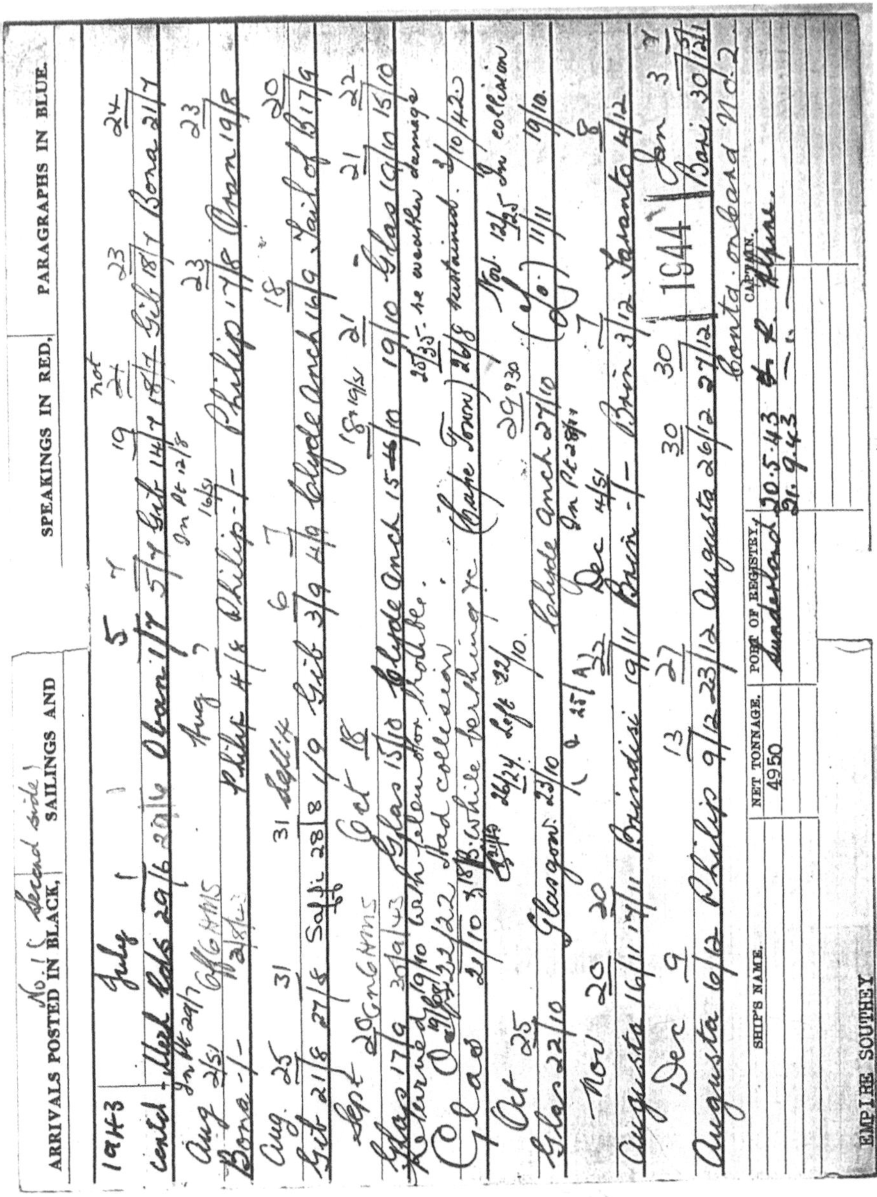

No. 1 (Second side)

ARRIVALS POSTED IN BLACK, SAILINGS AND SPEAKINGS IN RED, PARAGRAPHS IN BLUE.

1943 July

contd. Mersey Rds 29/6 20/6 Oban 1/7 5/7 Gib 14/7 18/7 Gib 18/7 Bona 21/7

Aug 2/51 Aug Bona -/- Philip 4/8 Philip -/- Philip 17/8 Oran 19/8

Aug 25 31 Sept 4 Gib 21/8 27/8 Saffi 28/8 1/9 Gib 3/9 4/9 Clyde Anch 16/9 Sail of B 17/9

Sept 20 Oct 18 Glas 17/9 30/9/43 Glas 15/10 Clyde Anch 15/10 19/10 Glas 19/10 15/10

Returned 19/10 with Helendoor Rolle, 25/3/5 re weather damage

Oct 22/22 had collision (Cape Town) 26/8 sustained 3/10/42

Glas 21/10 18/8 while berthing re. 26/24 Left 22/10 29/9/30 In collision

Oct 25 Glas 22/10 Glasgow 23/10 Clyde Anch 27/10 11/11 19/10

Nov 20 20 22 Dec 4/51

Augusta 16/11 17/11 Brindisi 19/11 Brin -/- Brin 3/12 Taranto 4/12

Dec 9 13 21 30 30 1944 Jan 3

Augusta 6/12 Philip 9/12 23/12 Augusta 26/12 27/12 Bari 30/12

Conta on board No. 2

SHIP'S NAME.	NET TONNAGE.	PORT OF REGISTRY.	CAPTAIN.
EMPIRE SOUTHEY	4950	Sunderland	30.5.43 / 21.9.43

ARRIVALS POSTED IN BLACK,   SAILINGS AND   SPEAKINGS IN RED,   PARAGRAPHS IN BLUE.

SHIP'S NAME.	NET TONNAGE.	PORT OF REGISTRY.	CAPTAIN.
CLAN COLQUHOUN	4888	Glasgow	5.10.42 A. J. Hogg.

P.T.O.

ARRIVALS POSTED IN BLACK,	SAILINGS AND	SPEAKINGS IN RED,	PARAGRAPHS IN BLUE.

1943 Contd.

June 12 July 5 9 12 Aug 5 9 11 17 Sept 1
Madras 10/6 Odl 2/7 7 Mall 9/7 3/8 Holsait 6/8 9/8 Prytt 14/8 28/8

Sept 25 27 30 Oct 7 13 14/9 Sw anything by fad
put in ... for

Balt 22/9 Crist 23/9 Key(?) 28/9 3/10 C. Henry 9/10 10. 13/10
(put in) 30/24 annual Newport 27/1.0
Oct 27/51 29/0

Norfolk 9/10 V ... Nov. 1 Nov. 3 18
Nov 19 26/2 21 Kamps 21.20/3
25/11 Zat raft. Homp Rds 26/10 N.Y. 31/10 Clyde Anch 17/11

Glas 17/11 Jan 1 Glas 30/12 Clyde Anch 30.31/12
Jan 3 3 18 Jel 1 (anch) 15 15 3
Jail of B. 30/12 Clyde Anch 31/12 Hal 10/1 30/1 Sw Bat 13/2 Sw 14/2 Feb 15/2 12/2 Damaged in Collision 12/2.
25 Apl 10 en Willington in gb. 15

Mat 9 10 12/24 15 (anch) 15 15 22 24
Lw 1/3 Mersey 8/3 N.Y. 8/3 4/5 6/7 V (anch) 13/5 Smd 13/5 14/5 Sw June 20/6 21/6

Apl 25 25 27 May 13 May 27
Matt Rds 23/4 23/4 Heam 24/4 de 25/4 de (c) 12/5 13/5 14/5 5 June 16/5 5
May 22 22 26 29 29 June 12/2 29 July 6
Mutt Rds 20/5 20/5 24/5 de 26/5 5 L 4/6 2 July 9/6 25/6 Grant B 2/7

June 20/5 Contd on card no 6

SHIP'S NAME.	NET TONNAGE.	PORT OF REGISTRY.	
CLAN COLQUHOUN	4888	Glasgow	14.12.43 O.J. Hogg CAPTAIN.

No. 8 (First side)

ARRIVALS POSTED IN BLACK. | SAILINGS AND | SPEAKINGS IN RED. | PARAGRAPHS IN BLUE.

SHIP'S NAME | NET TONNAGE | PORT OF REGISTRY
3936 | GLASGOW

1944

JMR
Department of National Defence

Naval Service

CANADA

IN REPLY PLEASE QUOTE.

No. XO - 3 - 7.

14th March, 1941

R.C.N. Barracks,
Halifax, N.S.

MRS.
~~Miss Ann~~ Douglas,
809 East Marquette Road,
Chicago, Illinois.

Dear Miss Douglas:

Your telegram of 4th March, 1941,
has been handed to me for investigation and reply.

I have made every endeavour to contact your
brother in the Merchant Ship which you have mentioned.
I have had no success in contacting him as yet but as
soon as his Ship makes her appearance in Halifax I
will communicate with you and inform him of the contents
of your wire.

Please be assured that everything possible
has been done in this Port and that we will continue
to do our utmost on your behalf.

K.F. Adams,
Commander, R.C.N.,
EXECUTIVE OFFICER.

DEPARTMENT OF STATE
WASHINGTON

In reply refer to
VD 811.111 Lucas, Andrew   August 18. 1943

My dear Mrs. Douglas:

    I have your letter of August 6, 1943 in further
reference to the case of your brother, Andrew Lucas,
whom you desire to have come to the United States for
a visit when his ship next reaches a Canadian port.

    As it appears from the information furnished by
you that your brother's case may fall within a category
which is exempted from the requirement of submitting
Forms BC to the Department for consideration of his
case under the centralized visa control procedure, I
have forwarded a copy of your letter under acknowledg-
ment, as well as a copy of your previous communication
of July 12, 1943, to the American Consul at St. John,
New Brunswick, with a request that he submit a report
to the Department of what the records of his office
indicate in the matter. Upon the receipt of a reply
I shall communicate further with you.

                Sincerely yours,

H. K. Travers
Chief, Visa Division

Mrs. Nan Douglas,
      11113 South Hayne Avenue,
         Chicago, Illinois.

The War Years (1939-45)
(f) The Deserter

After changing ships again, Andrew arrived in Halifax, Nova Scotia, Canada aboard the SS Colquhoun on Christmas Eve 1943. Having managed to evade the German U-boats and aircraft on the dreaded Atlantic crossing, the mood on board the ship on that Christmas Eve was one of relief at survival and jubilation at some well earned rest.

For the crew in general and for Andrew in particular, this was just one of the many hazardous trips across the Atlantic that they would make during the Second World War. These trips were to be euphemistically called 'The Atlantic Convoy'. Depending on which 'convoy' a ship was assigned to would also depend on whether that ship was more vulnerable to attack. Some ships were assigned to the Slow Convoy (SC) due to the nature and size of the ship. On this occasion Andrew's ship was not on an SC convoy.

The festive celebrations lasted well into the night and most of Christmas Day. The comfort and 'safety' of Halifax was a welcome break and with some minor repairs to be carried out and the SS Colquhoun reloaded, the ship was not due to sail until the middle of January. The New Year celebrations proved to be a drunken affair and a time to forget, albeit temporarily, the forthcoming perilous return across the Atlantic.

Just a few days later Andrew made a monumental decision, which could have potentially changed his life for ever. Despite some intermittent contact with his family, Andrew had not seen them in over 20 years. He was now 24 and despite being abandoned by them as a toddler, Andrew had a strong urge to go and see them.

He knew the address of their home in Chicago, but had no real idea of how he would get there from Canada, or how long it would take him. At 6am on the cold morning of 4th January, 1944, while most of the ship's crew were asleep, Andrew gathered some clothes into his seaman's kitbag and left the SS Colquhoun in search of his family. Armed with the telegram, showing the family address, which his sister had sent to congratulate him and Mary Frances on their wedding, he headed out of the dockyard.

The distance from Halifax to Chicago is some 1,224 miles *(see map)*. Andrew passed through the dockyard security with no problem after showing his docking pass, but the options after that were pretty limited. He could not drive and the cost of flying was too expensive. That left only the train or hitching a lift.

As Andrew had no immigration papers, he would not be allowed into the USA so would have to enter illegally. He also had to bear in mind that he would have to be back before his ship sailed back across the Atlantic.

Andrew searched the docks looking for a truck which was going south as near as possible to the USA. Due to the increased traffic because of the war, Andrew found a truck driver who was going to Maine, just over the US border.

During the journey, Andrew, in his strong Irish accent, admitted to the driver where he was

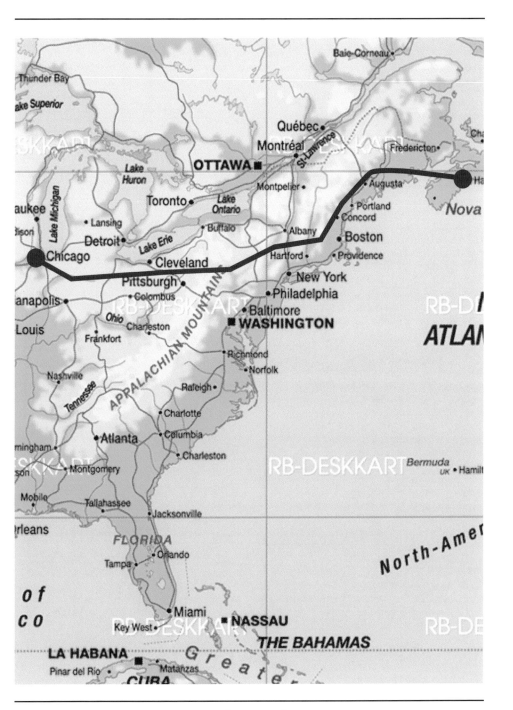

heading and that he did not have the necessary papers, visa or passes to get into the US. The driver advised Andrew to hide in the back of his truck when they approached the border, because things had changed in America due to the war and the country had tightened up on all its border crossings.

The US feared that illegal aliens would enter the country and undermine their security, so by 1942 the Border Patrol had increased its agents to 1531. The Border Patrol's specific remit was to tighten control of the crossings, provide security for detention camps for aliens, and to assist the US Coastguard in searching for spies. They had also started to use aircraft for the first time to assist them in their hunt for spies, so it was against this backdrop that Andrew attempted to enter the US illegally.

However, as luck would have it the border crossing went without a hitch. The familiarity of the truck drivers and the constant flow of traffic made the Border Patrol agents lax and disinterested, so a cursory glance allowed Andrew to enter the US.

Having survived the crossing, Andrew was deposited outside Maine at a roadside café, frequented by many of the truck drivers. With so many vehicles it was hard for Andrew to decide how best to go about getting his next lift. Ignoring the stares given to any stranger, Andrew took at seat at the counter and ordered some breakfast. With his unusual and distinctive accent he soon attracted some attention from other customers and lorry drivers.

Before long Andrew had made contact with a lorry driver who was going all the way to New York, a place which he had visited before so was familiar with its docks. The distance from Maine to New York is some 450 miles. After eating his breakfast, Andrew took his seat beside the driver and they headed on down to New York – a journey of almost 12 hours, with a couple of stops on the way.

Some time during the day of the 5th January, they arrived in New York and Andrew thanked the driver then made his way to the Manhattan dock area. During this time New York Harbour was divided into 600 individual ship anchorages, able to accommodate ships berthing or awaiting convoy assignments. On a peak day during WW2, there were a total of some 543 merchant ships at anchor in New York Harbour.

Having visited New York previously, Andrew made his way to the waterfront of Manhattan and checked into a seedy dockside hotel where no questions were asked and nobody cared. He went down to the harbour area to look for a lift out of New York to Chicago, then returned to his hotel and spent a very restless night.

He awoke very early on the morning of the 6th January – the second day of his desertion. Dispensing with the hotel's breakfast, Andrew made his way to the docks. With so much coming and going and so many ships loading and unloading, Andrew found his way to the main terminal where the loaded trucks departed. Finding a truck heading in the direction of Chicago was not that difficult.

The Port of New York handled some 3million troops and their equipment and over 63 million tons of additional supplies and materials from1942-1945. The hustle and bustle of the harbour made it easy for Andrew to move around without attracting attention. By this time the Captain of his ship docked in Nova Scotia had already notified the authorities of his absence, and a warrant had been issued for his arrest by the RCMP (Royal Canadian Mounted Police). The US Immigration and Border Patrol had also been notified. Andrew was now officially classified as a 'deserter'.

After several hours of searching for a lift to Chicago, Andrew realised that a one-stop lift was going to be nearly impossible. With a distance from New York to Chicago of some 788 miles, he decided that he would have to alter his journey. After consulting a map of the USA, he reckoned that a lift to or near Pennsylvania would be a good move, and from there he could get a lift to Indiana, with a final lift from Indiana to Chicago. This journey would take at least one or two days, if he was lucky. What Andrew had not considered was how he was going to get back to Halifax and re-join his ship before it departed for Britain on the 14th of January, nor what kind of reception he was likely to receive at his parents' home. For the moment his uppermost thoughts were of seeing his mother and father. He had come too far to turn back.

At around midday on the 6th January, Andrew struck lucky. Amidst all the hustle and bustle of New York Harbour, he found a truck driver who was returning to Ohio after delivering wartime materials. Once aboard the truck Andrew proceeded to relate his story to the driver who found it so preposterous that he believed him. The road to Pennsylvania/ Ohio is some 370 miles. With several stops along the way the journey to Pennsylvania/ Ohio took the best part of 12 hours and was pleasant although very cold. With no heating in the truck, the cold winter air could be felt in the cabin.

In the very early hours of the morning of the 7th January, Andrew was dropped off on the outskirts of Ohio near a cheap motel. He checked in but slept lightly. He had to get up early to find another lift that would take him on his final leg of his journey to Chicago, or as near to there as possible.

Later that morning Andrew was given directions by the staff at the motel where to find the main truck distribution centre. He knew that if there was a chance of a lift it would be at one of those centres, rather than waiting on the nearest highway. The weather was turning colder by the day, and it was already around -7 degrees with the strong possibility of snow.

Finding his way to the main war distribution centre from where materials were transported to and from Ohio to Chicago and New York, Andrew sought out a haulage firm which regularly used the Chicago-Ohio-New York route. He found a truck which was already loaded and ready to leave for Chicago – the final leg of his journey. With some 351 miles to travel from Ohio to Chicago, the trip was likely to take between eight and ten hours.

Andrew quickly struck up a good relationship with the driver. In each case when he had told his story, all the drivers who helped him had been amazed and overwhelmed at the trip he was undertaking. And each one was so impressed that they were only too happy to help him.

The journey from Ohio to Chicago passed quite quickly with a couple of stops along the way, but eventually the weary passenger was dropped at around midnight as close as the driver could go to Andrew's parents' house. The driver said that a short taxi ride would take him to 6241 Southpark.

After exchanging farewells Andrew hailed a taxi for the short 10 minute journey to his parent's house. He had no idea what kind of reception he would receive from his family, as he had not notified them in advance that he was coming. Despite some intermittent contact over the years, Andrew still harboured a feeling of having been abandoned and had some questions that he wanted to ask his parents.

As the taxi drove up to the given address, it was dark and hard to make out the house numbers and names. After paying the taxi driver, Andrew walked up the driveway to his parents' house. With his kitbag over his shoulder, Andrew approached the house. A knot of anxiety, fear, hope, excitement and trepidation was running through his stomach. His heart rate was getting quicker and he began to sweat.

There was a light on inside the house, which meant that somebody was still awake. He took a sharp intake of breath and knocked on the door. He could hear muffled voices and people talking. Time seemed to stand still as he waited for someone to come to the door. As with most security-conscious American householders, there were many locks on the door. Eventually the main door opened slightly, and a female voice asked who was there.

Andrew explained who he was and who he was looking for but, because the area was in darkness, she asked him to show her some identification. He produced his seaman's card and handed it in. The door closed and a few minutes later there was a loud cry of excitement and joy. The main door flew open and Andrew's sister Nan threw herself at him, crying, and nearly knocked him off his feet. The rest of the family appeared and joined in, then took Andrew into the living room where he embraced his mother. They stood quietly for several minutes, both of them and his father crying. It seemed like hours before anyone would let go.

Back in Canada the hunt for Andrew had intensified, as he was now officially classified as a deserter. The consequences for him, if found, would be grave; in all likelihood he could end up in one of America's detention camps. As he told his tale about the journey to his family, Andrew realised that he could not spend too much time with them. He would have to go back to Nova Scotia and rejoin his ship before the 14th, but it would take him the best part of two days to get back to Halifax.

Andrew spent two days with his family and on the morning of the 10th January, they took him to the train station in Chicago, insisting on paying for his train fare to New York and giving him enough money to buy a train ticket from New York to Maine.

Having to say goodbye to his family was tearful and heart-wrenching. As he stood on the platform with his arms round his mother, neither of them wanted to let go. The final whistle sounded and Andrew pulled himself from his mother and boarded the train. The promise to write was made and the commitment to return guaranteed, but it would be the first and the last time that Andrew would see his family. He never revealed whatever information he discovered about why he had been abandoned in childhood, but clearly some form of reconciliation had taken place. His mother died in 1946.

Once the train pulled away from the station, Andrew settled down to some peace and quite and some reflective thinking. The train journey from Chicago to New York was pleasant enough, although Andrew took very little notice of the countryside as his thoughts were elsewhere. The journey was a lot less arduous that the countless lifts and freezing cold that he had endured getting to Chicago, but his mind was racing about what would happen when he reached Halifax.

He knew that he would be in trouble – by now he had been posted missing for over a week. However he comforted himself with the fact that he had managed to see his mother and father for the first time in almost 20 years. He believed that whatever punishment he would receive was worth that.

Eventually the train arrived in New York Central Station. Andrew's next task was to find out how he would get a connection to Canada. After seeking some help at the Information counter, he was advised to take a train to Maine, go through the border crossing then get a connection to New Brunswick and finally a connection to Halifax.

Andrew had to spend the night of the 11th January sleeping in Grand Central Station as the next connection to Maine was not until the following morning. Catching only some fitful sleep during the night, Andrew finally boarded the train heading for Maine, settled back and immediately tiredness overcame him. Some time later he was awakened by the sound of the ticket collector checking all the passengers and their tickets.

The train finally stopped at Maine and Andrew had to depart along with everyone else and go through the Border crossing. With no US visa or documentation other than his seaman's discharge book, Andrew realised that he would have to report to the authorities. He could not evade the Border Patrol or the Immigration authorities, so he presented himself to the Border Patrol agents and effectively 'gave himself up'.

After some deliberation Andrew was taken away for questioning while the Border Patrol agents investigated his story. As he was on their list as a 'British deserter', he spent the night in a detention centre while the authorities decided what to do with him. They contacted their equivalent authorities in Canada and, because Andrew was a British citizen, it was decided that the Royal Canadian Mountain Police would come and collect him.

On the morning of the 13th January Andrew was collected by two RCMP officers and driven back across the Canadian border to New Brunswick. There he was held in detention for a further two days while the Canadian authorities and the British Consulate debated what to do with him. By now his ship had left Halifax and was on its way back to Britain, so Andrew had literally missed his boat.

He was interrogated, his story was collaborated and in addition the US authorities visited his parents' house in Chicago to verify his statement. Eventually because he was badly needed for the merchant ships during the war, and having missed his boat, he was put on the Canadian Merchant Navy Reserve list and assigned to the first available ship heading back to the UK.

He was also exonerated and the 'deserter' stigma lifted because he voluntarily returned. Once again the dreaded call of an Atlantic Convoy awaited him. In his discharge book it is clearly stated that he was wanted by a Mr. Bryant and identified as a deserter, but this has been crossed out and the word 'exonerated' inserted instead. If Andrew had not rejoined the war effort he would not have been entitled to claim any of the five medals to which he was entitled.

The War Years (1939-45)
(g) Injustice

The Battle of the Atlantic, according to Winston Churchill, was the Battle FOR Britain. However it should be noted that Merchant Seaman received NO paid leave when they returned to port. If they wished to spend some time with their families they had to sign off from ship and go without pay.

Incredibly, under British law, if a ship went down, the obligation of the ship's owners to the crew also went down with it. Should a Merchant Seaman go down with his ship, his relatives would – unless the seaman was assigned to a more generous shipping line – receive NO pay from the day he died. A Merchant Seaman's wages stopped when his ship went down, and a Merchant Seaman's contract ended when a torpedo or bomb struck. Yet there was a distinct lack of lifesaving equipment on board many of the ships.

Protests by the Merchant Seaman's Union and other trade unions were not listened to about this injustice. It was not until May 1941, some three years into the war, that the Government introduced the 'Essential Work Order', thereby rectifying a terrible injustice.
So it was a great surprise, and a welcome relief, when Andrew received a letter dated 17/4/1942 from the shipping line Cayzer Irvine, enclosing a cheque for £3 in recognition of his contribution to the company during the 'difficulties' of the war. A copy of the letter is attached. Needless to say, not all the shipping lines were as generous.

In May 1945, the Second World War ended.

Chapter 6

The Post War Years (1945 – 1959)

After the end of the Second World War Andrew returned to peacetime seafaring. The aftermath of the war had taken its toll on the whole country.

Gradually but slowly life was beginning to get back to normal. Still staying in a room and kitchen in 20 Thornhill Street, Parkhead, Glasgow, Andrew and Mary restarted their married life. For the first three years that they were married, their life had been filled with uncertainty and doubt. Mary had been left alone for long periods of time, always wondering if Andrew would return home safely.

However the end of hostilities signalled a new start and a new family. The year the war ended saw Mary give birth to their first born baby, a son. As was the custom in those days, he was named after his father, Andrew.

After taking some small jobs at home Andrew eventually returned to sea in early 1946. It was to be an eventful year for him in many ways.

By the 4th February, he had joined the Imperial Transport ship and completed a short

CAYZER, IRVINE & CO. LTD

MANAGERS OF

THE CLAN LINE STEAMERS LTD.

LONDON, GLASGOW & LIVERPOOL.

TELEGRAMS:
"CAYZER, HOOK, HANTS"
"CAYZER, GLASGOW"
"CAYZER, LIVERPOOL"

OUR REFCE

YOUR "

TELEPHONE HOOK 168 (3 LINES)

TYLNEY HALL,

ROTHERWICK,

BASINGSTOKE, HANTS.

17th April 1942.

Dear Sir,

The past year was another one of difficulty with the continuation of hostilities, which have even become more widespread, but, notwithstanding this, our confidence in ultimate victory remains unshaken.

We appreciate highly the continued loyal co-operation of our sea-going and shore staffs and it has again been decided to give suitable expression of this. We therefore enclose cheque for £3......, as a special bonus and should be glad if you would receipt and return relative credit note.

Yours faithfully,

per pro CAYZER, IRVINE & CO. LTD.,

General Manager.

Mr. A. Lucas.
146, Quarryknowie Street,
Parkhead,
Glasgow.

TELEPHONE HOOK 168 (3 LINES)

TYLNEY HALL,
ROTHERWICK,
BASINGSTOKE, HANTS.

CAYZER, IRVINE & CO. LTD.
MANAGERS OF
THE CLAN LINE STEAMERS LTD.
LONDON, GLASGOW & LIVERPOOL.

TELEGRAMS:
"CAYZER, HOOK, HANTS"
"CAYZER, GLASGOW"
"CAYZER, LIVERPOOL"

OUR REFCE

YOUR "

17th April 1942.

Dear Sir,

The past year was another one of difficulty with the continuation of hostilities, which have even become more widespread, but, notwithstanding this, our confidence

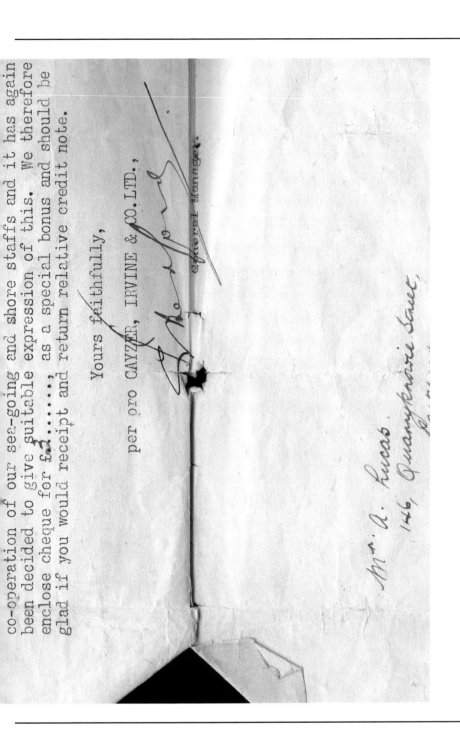

co-operation of our sea-going and shore staffs and it has again
been decided to give suitable expression of this. We therefore
enclose cheque for £......, as a special bonus and should be
glad if you would receipt and return relative credit note.

Yours faithfully,

per pro CAYZER, IRVINE & CO. LTD.,

General Manager.

Mr A. Lucas.
146 Quaybridge Lane,

LUCAS

Andrew Lucas, beloved husband of the late Elizabeth, nee McCallion; loving father of Nan (Joe) Douglas, John, Andrew (Mary) of Glasgow, Scotland, Thomas, Marie (Si) Savino and Elaine Lucas; dear grandfather of 23; also survived by many great-grandchildren, nieces and nephews. Native of Glasgow, Scotland. Funeral Thursday, 8:45 a.m., from The Chapel, 2100 W. 95th St. at Hoyne, to St. Barnabas Church. Mass 9:30 a.m. Interment Holy Sepulchre. Visitation 2-10 p.m. Wednesday. 779-3535.

"we have loved her in life,
let us not forget her in death"
—St. Augustine.

O Compassionate Lord Jesus
grant her eternal rest.—7
years and 7 quarantines.

Crucifie Lord Jesus, have
me, cy on her soul.

In Loving Memory
OF
ELIZABETH LUCAS
INGLESIDE AVENUE,
Who died on 9th December, 1946
R. I. P.

GENTLEST and Most
Merciful Heart of Jesus
ever present in the Blessed
Sacrament, ever consumed
with burning love for the poor
captive souls in P...

engagement which ended on 8th May. After a three-day break he joined the Norvegian and stayed with her until 16th September. On December 9 that year Andrew's mother, Elizabeth Lucas died in Chicago, and Andrew was devastated that he could not get to her funeral. However he consoled himself that he had finally been reconciled with her during his visit in 1944. For the next six years Andrew would work and sail the coast of the UK. However as the increase in the demand for goods and materials grew, there was a great expansion of the Merchant Navy. Ships became bigger and the lure of more money became too great to resist.

By 1952 he was the father of Andrew, John, Thomas, Mary and Ann. With the family still cramped in a slum dwelling in 20 Thornhill Street, Andrew decided that he needed to do more long haulage trips to earn enough money to feed his young family.

On the 1st July, 1950 Andrew joined the SS Cortona and stayed with her until 31st March the following year, then had a two month break at home. He did not really enjoy the living accommodation that his family had to endure at 20 Thornhill Street, deciding instead to spend a large part of his time at 146 Quarryknowe Street and O'Kanes pub!! On the 19th March, 1951 Andrew re-joined the Laurentia and sailed with her until 16th August, joining the SS Maidenhead two days later, where he was promoted to Bosun.

He finished his stay with the Maidenhead on 2nd April 1952 and less than three weeks later joined the Corona on a short engagement until 27th May. An even shorter engagement saw Andrew join the Linguist on the 28th May and disembark from her exactly one month later.

On the 30th June 1952 Andrew joined the Fidra for a short engagement until 8th August and at the end of that month he had joined the ESSO Belfast until 8th October. Staying with the ESSO company, Andrew joined the ESSO Hull On 10th December and finished his engagement with her on 24th June 1953 where he discharged at Tilbury docks in London.

After a month at home, Andrew joined the SS Findhorn on 21th July 1953. However a severe accident at work almost killed him. During a heavy storm, Andrew had gone to check the cargo and found himself thrown down into the cargo hold. On returning to shore he was temporarily employed ashore because he was declared medically unfit for sea service (see discharge papers). Unfortunately for Andrew he received no compensation for this accident, and his injuries would return to haunt him in his later years.

By October 1953 Andrew had joined the SS Barren Hill bound for Panama, discharging on her return to Southampton on November 19. At the end of that month he joined the M.V. Diplomat in Manchester and discharged on the 2nd December.

On 4th December Andrew was given permission to join the SS Cornel for a short home voyage to Garston, arriving on 10th December. On the 14th he stepped on board the SS Shuna for a foreign trip, discharging on its return to Glasgow on 19th January 1954. After a 10 day stay at home Andrew joined the SS Lestris on 29th January for a short trip to Liverpool.

The SS Kirkwood was his next ship, boarding on 19th February at Sunderland and eventually docking in North Shields on the 24th. The SS Orchy was his next ship, embarking on 1st March until 7th May, and for the next 16 months Andrew enjoyed the luxury of sailing close to home. The furthest he would travel to was Middlesbrough.

Andrew had a short trip on his next ship, the M.V. Crane – a 165376 tonnes out of London. Then on the 23rd July Andrew joined the SS Avis – a 166054 tonne out of London – as a Bosun, disembarking on the 18th October. Once again Andrew achieved a 'very good' for his ability and general conduct.

From the 1st to the 22nd of November Andrew was on the M.V. Sanda, an 1190 tonne out of Glasgow. After a short home leave, he joined the SS Beauly on 6th December and stayed with her until 19th January1955, transferring immediately to R.F.A. Sea Fox, with a 33,354 tonnes, disembarking at the end of the engagement on 16th February.

On the 22nd February Andrew left Glasgow on the Lairdshill and continued to sail with her until 30th September, then on October 1st he had a short voyage on the SS San Casto – a 2526 tonne from the port of London – and disembarked from her on 15th October. Six days later Andrew joined the SS Holdenmore in Glasgow, docking in Newcastle on 31st October and on 11th November he joined the SS Alpera in Glasgow and sailed with her to Genoa in Italy, returning to Glasgow on 6th December.

On the 14th December Andrew joined the SS Saint Conan until he left her on 30th December. After a very short New Year break at home Andrew joined the SS Brora – a 1028 tonne out of Glasgow – on 4th January until the 17th, and on the 29th he joined the M.V. Redefield – a 183361 tonne out of Newcastle – at Bowling, leaving her on 10th February 1956.

On the 20th February Andrew joined the M.V. Esso Plymouth and landed at Manchester on March 4th. The following day he joined the SS Girasol and left her on March 28th, joining the M.V. Lady Anstruther – a 317 tonne out of Glasgow – the following week, eventually docking at Irvine on 20th April. After a short shore leave Andrew joined the SS Lady Dorothy – a 578 tonne out of Glasgow – on 30th April and discharged from her on 14th May at Irvine dock. At the Broomielaw, Glasgow, Andrew joined the Tamaroa on 19th May and sailed with her from Glasgow to Liverpool arriving two days later.

A foreign trip was next as Andrew joined the SS Corinthian – a 3198 tonne out of Liverpool – at Glasgow on 24th May and docked back in Liverpool on 25th July. Returning to Glasgow Andrew then joined the Invertset docked in Bowling on 1st August, remaining with her for the full month.

After another short home break, Andrew was on his travels again. This time he joined the ESSO Tioga – a 797 tonne out of Grangemouth – at Bowling, returning there on November 3rd. Once again his Discharge Book testifies that Andrew achieved a 'very good' for his ability and 'very good' for his conduct.

Andrew stayed with the ESSO Tioga until she returned to Bowling on 11th January 1957, then enjoyed a three day home pass before rejoining the ESSO Tioga, returning once again to Bowling on 20th March. On the 27th March Andrew joined the M.V. Loch Broom – a 324 tonne out of Glasgow – until 4th May, then had a 10 day home leave before joining the M. V. Loch Dunvegan – a 528 tonne out of Glasgow – from May 14th until June 25th.

Immediately after leaving the Loch Dunvegan, Andrew joined the SS Loch Frisa – a 239 tonne out of Glasgow – for a short trip, until July 5th, then re-joined the M.V. Loch Dunvegan on

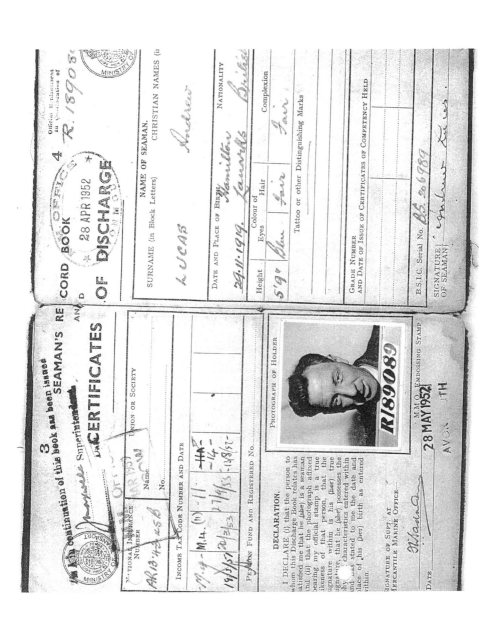

9th July until the 22nd. Andrew then returned to the Invertest on 29th July at Bowling until 1st August, and three days later joined the M. V. Sanda – an 853 tonne out of Glasgow – until September 9th.

On the 16th September Andrew joined the M.V. Raeburn – a 8312 tonne out of Liverpool – for only two days, then went to join the M.V. Sydney Star, –a 6795 tonne out of Belfast – and sailed with her to Antwerp, arriving on 24th September.

By this time Andrew was employed as a Lamptrimmer and as an Able Bodied Seaman. He then returned home to his family for a well-earned break, staying for almost six weeks – one of the longest periods he ever spent at home. By this time he had a family of six children and conditions at home were not great.

It was during this period in his life that Andrew decided to try and find suitable employment ashore. With a young, growing family Andrew realised he was missing too much of their childhood. Mary was virtually a single, mother having to look after the six children on her own.

The housing conditions were terrible. Living in a slum single-end meant that the house was cramped, with only room for one bed and a bed recess. There was no hot running water, only a cold tap. There was no inside toilet, and Maryused a zinc bath to wash all the children. The back-court was rat infested and it became quite clear that they could not stay at 20 Thornhill Street for much longer.

As much as Andrew tried to find work, he had been at sea most of his life and it was the only job he knew. So on the 6th November he joined the M.V. Geelong – an 8453 tonne out of London – in Liverpool and sailed on foreign trips until 19th February. By this time Andrew was now a Bosun, AB and a Lamptrimmer.

Returning for another eight week stay, Andrew found the conditions at home were now unbearable for his young family. Although they had put their name down for a Glasgow Corporation House, nothing was forthcoming. The rat-infested backcourt, coupled with the cramped living accommodation – one bed for 6 children, a bed recess for him and Mary, and an outside toilet – put a considerable strain on the family.

At that time the city fathers were contemplating pulling down the houses in a slum -clearance programme and rehousing people outside the city – but that would be at least a year away. In the meantime Andrew once again looked for alternative employment, but his long years in the Merchant Navy went against him.

So on April 10th, 1958 Andrew rejoined the SS Laurentia and sailed to Montreal, Canada, arriving there on 10th May. He was to make 11 voyages across the Atlantic with the Laurentia to Montreal, Canada, eventually disembarking from her on 14th May in Glasgow, as a Lamptrimmer. After a one week stay at home, Andrew joined the SS Marylyn – a 4458 tonne out of London – at the Broomielaw, Glasgow and set sail for Rotterdam.

Andrew stayed with the SS Marylyn until 27th October and on returning to Glasgow, joined the SS Baron Cawdor – a 3720 tonne out of Ardrossan – completing a foreign trip on 22nd

The Donaldson Line of Steamers.

S.S. Laurentia

DONALDSON BROS. & BLACK, LTD.
Managers.

Port of Glasgow. 15 March 1950

To whom it may concern,

This certifies that Mr A. Lucas is regularly employed on this vessel on the Glasgow – Montreal service and I recommend him as being a reliable and trustworthy employee of this company, always sober and attentive to his duties.

[signature]
Master

December. Andrew then spent the end of the decade at home – one of his rare Christmases with his wife and children. It was also the first Christmas that Andrew and his family spent in their new home at 122 Wellhouse Crescent – one of the new homes built by the Corporation of Glasgow as part of their slum clearance programme.

The area was called Easterhouse and the new housing scheme was situated out in the 'country' some four miles from Parkhead and Shettleston. On that first Christmas in Easterhouse, the family enjoyed the comfort of four bedrooms, an inside toilet and hot and cold running water – sheer luxury!

Having spent the festive season with his wife and children Andrew started the new decade off by joining the SS Alhama – an 1169 tonne out of Glasgow – and returned to Glasgow after a foreign trip on 25th February 1960. On the 4th March he joined the M.V. Emerald – a 1454 tonne out of Glasgow – in Blythe and left her on 17th April.

He rejoined the Emerald in Ardrossan on 16th August for a foreign trip and disembarked from her some five months later on 7th January 1961, in Middlesborough. Andrew then made his way back to Glasgow for a short home leave. On the 9th February he joined the SS Cameo – a 1597 tonne out of Glasgow – in Londonderry, Northern Ireland, and returned to Belfast on 2nd May, after completing several foreign trips.

After another short home leave, Andrew rejoined the SS Cameo on 22nd May and returned to Troon on 8th August, after completing a foreign trip. A three week home visit this time and then Andrew joined the M.V. Turquoise – a 550 tonne – in Londonderry on 6th September, returning to Ayr on 17th November. The next ship would be the M.V. Amethyst – a 1547 tonne – which he joined in Goole on 27th November and disembarked in Belfast on December 11th, by which time he was a Bosun.

Unfortunately yet another Christmas and New Year was spent away from his family, but at least he had the comfort of knowing that they were now living in better conditions. During his time with the Amethyst, Andrew made four long foreign trips, lasting over 12 months.

A well-earned stay at home allowed Andrew the unexpected luxury of spending Christmas of 1962 and the New Year with his family, whom he had not seen in over a year. Returning to sea he joined the M.V. Topaz – a 1596 tonne – in Belfast on 27th January 1963, returning to Londonderry on 2nd March. On returning to Glasgow, Andrew joined the SS Baron Inverclyde – a 5478 tonne out of Ardrossan – on 25th March for a foreign trip, finishing back at Ardrossan on 14th May.

After a 12 day home break, Andrew joined the M.V. Prase – a 374 tonne out of Glasgow – on 27th May, eventually returning to Belfast on 21st May, 1965 – some 2 years later!! In that time Andrew, now a qualified Bosun, had only managed home for two short breaks. He then joined the M.V. Turquoise on 1st July, leaving her on 21st December for another rare festive break at home with his family.

Once again Andrew tried to find work at home as his family were growing up and he had missed so much of their early childhood. But six months later, despite several attempts at finding suitable employment on land, Andrew gave in and returned to sea.

On the 18th July 1966 he joined the M.V. Sicilia – a 6120 tonne – at the Broomielaw, Glasgow. Andrew completed four foreign trips with her, leaving on 15th January 1967 after six months at sea. After a four week lay off, he joined the Royal Ulsterman – a 1449 tonne – on 4th March until 15th April, then the M.V. Tourmaline – an 854 tonne – from June 11 until he disembarked in Belfast on August 14.

On that last voyage the ship ran into a severe storm, and Andrew had gone down into the cargo hold to examine the merchandise which the Tourmaline was carrying, as there was a danger of the cargo breaking free. While he was descending the steps to the cargo hold, a huge swell smashed into the boat, pushing her almost onto her side. Andrew was flung off the steps and landed badly, breaking his collarbone and severely damaging his arm.

Hospitalisation was out of the question as the ship was at sea, so instead a very crude first aid was applied. Unfortunately, by the time Andrew arrived back on dry land, he was in a pretty bad shape. This was to prove the start of his decline and eventual demise. For as well as having to deal with his broken arm and collarbone, Andrew then contracted tuberculosis due to his heavy smoking. For the next two years he was in considerable pain and unemployed, receiving little help or assistance either from his employers or from his trade union, the National Union of Seamen (NUS).

During 1969 Andrew made a sufficient recovery to be able to get back to work, but the thought of working on dry land did not appeal to him. Once again the lure of the sea was calling and on 22nd December he boarded the M.V. Amber – a 1596 tonne – out of Glasgow, for a foreign trip returning to dock in Liverpool on 25th March, 1970. After a two month break, Andrew rejoined her on 12th May in Ayr, finally leaving her in Belfast on 14/12/1970.

Unfortunately Andrew's ill health returned and it was clear he would not be able to embark on foreign trips any more. Facing a medical, it was decided that he should transfer to the ferry ship sailing from Stranraer to Belfast.

He joined the British Transport Ship on 23rd March 1971 until 16th January 1972 and, after a six week lay off, Andrew returned to the Stranraer ferry on 6th March.

On the 4th May, 1972, Andrew Lucas, R189089, AB, Bosun, Lamptrimmer, Lifeboatman, and Mess Boy, completed his last seafaring journey. In his discharge book his report on his ability was 'very good' and his conduct 'very good', as it had been throughout his 30 odd years at sea. Andrew Lucas was medically retired - an inglorious end to a fascinating life at sea.

Chapter 7

The Move to Easterhouse - 1959

Back in 1959 Andrew, Mary and their six children were still living in damp, overcrowded conditions. The couple had been living in 20 Thornhill Street since they were married in 1942, with conditions becoming more cramped and squalid over the past 15 years.

As they, like many others, had put their names down for a Corporation house, it was a question of patiently waiting until they reached the top of the queue. Glasgow was about to undergo a massive slum clearance programme, and by the mid-1950's new houses were beginning to be built in the outskirts of the city.

Andrew and Mary's single-end flat, which had no inside toilet or hot and cold running water, was no place to bring up a growing family. The backcourt was rat-infested, and the Andrews shelter, a relic from WW2, was still standing.

However things were about to change. Andrew and Mary received a letter from the Corporation of Glasgow advising them that they qualified for a new house on the outskirts of the city, in a place called Easterhouse. The letter contained directions and bus routes and they were advised to report at a certain location to draw lots as to which new house they would get.

Andrew and Mary left the family with Granny Gibson and headed for Easterhouse. A Wee 30 bus took them to Wellhouse, Easterhouse, where they met other 'settlers' from different parts of the city, and Andrew and Mary drew number 122 Wellhouse Crescent.

The whole area was still a large building site, with many of the houses yet to be completed. The so-called five apartment townhouses were complete and would house all the families with

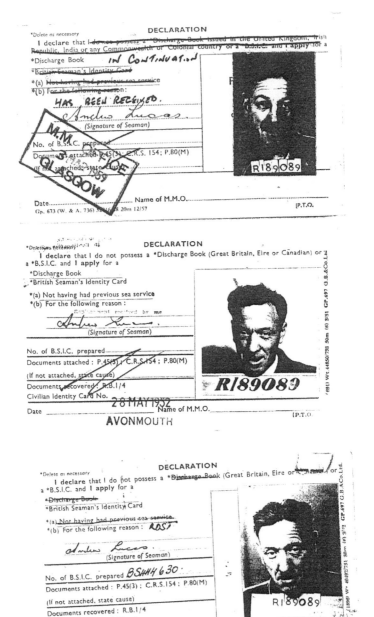

DECLARATION

I declare that I ~~do not possess a~~ *Discharge Book issued in the United Kingdom, Irish Republic, India or any Commonwealth or Colonial country or a B.S.I.C. and I apply for a

*Discharge Book   *IN CONTINUATION*

*~~British Seaman's Identity Card~~

*(a) ~~Not having had previous sea service~~
*(b) ~~For the following reason~~:

HAS BEEN RECEIVED.

Andrew Lucas
(Signature of Seaman)

No. of B.S.I.C. prepared
Documents attached : P.45(3) ; C.R.S. 154 ; P.80(M)
(If not attached, state cause)

Date.................................. Name of M.M.O..............................
Gp. 673 (W. & A. 736) [illegible] 20m 12/57   [P.T.O.

DECLARATION

*Delete as necessary
I declare that I do not possess a *Discharge Book (Great Britain, Eire or Canadian) or a *B.S.I.C. and I apply for a

*Discharge Book
*British Seaman's Identity Card

*(a) Not having had previous sea service
*(b) For the following reason :
Replacement received by me

Andrew Lucas
(Signature of Seaman)

No. of B.S.I.C. prepared
Documents attached : P.45(3) ; C.R.S.154 ; P.80(M)
(If not attached, state cause)
Documents recovered : R.B.1/4
Civilian Identity Card No.

Date _____ 28 MAY 1952 _____ Name of M.M.O. _____   [P.T.O.

AVONMOUTH

DECLARATION

*Delete as necessary
I declare that I do not possess a *~~Discharge Book~~ (Great Britain, Eire or [illegible]) or a *B.S.I.C. and I apply for a

*~~Discharge Book~~
*British Seaman's Identity Card

*(a) ~~Not having had previous sea service~~
*(b) For the following reason : LOST

Andrew Lucas
(Signature of Seaman)

No. of B.S.I.C. prepared BS444 630
Documents attached : P.45(3) ; C.R.S.154 ; P.80(M)
(If not attached, state cause)
Documents recovered : R.B.1/4
Civilian Identity Card No.

Date 28/7/54.   Name of M.M.O. Glasgow   [P.T.O.

Exn. 50B

APPLICATION FOR A CERTIFICATE OF COMPETENCY AS A.B. BY A PERSON CLAIMING ENTITLEMENT UNDER REGULATION 4 OF THE MERCHANT SHIPPING

(CERTIFICATES OF COMPETENCY AS A.B.) REGULATIONS, 1952

MERCHANT SHIPPING ACT, 1948

N.B.—Certificates of discharge or other evidence proving sea service shown in Part B must be lodged with the Superintendent. Service entered in Part B must have been performed as A.B. or in an equivalent or superior deck rating on or before 1st May, 1952, in a ship for which an agreement with the crew was required under Part II of the Merchant Shipping Act, 1894.

PART A. Name, etc. of Applicant

Surname (in block letters) _LUCAS_ Other names _ANDREW_

Date and place of birth _29.11.1919 HAMILTON_ Nationality _BRITISH_

No. of Discharge Book _R.189089_ Present Rating _Jan_

Height _5_ ft. _9_ ins. Colour of Eyes _Blue_ Hair _Jan_ Complexion _Jan_

Tattoo or other marks (if any) _____

PART B. Declaration to be made by Applicant

I hereby declare that I served in the rating of _AB._ in the _Cortona_

a seagoing vessel of _8789_ tons from _22.4._ 19_52_

to _27.5_ 19_52_ and I hereby apply for a Certificate of Competency as A.B.

to be issued to me through the Mercantile Marine Office at _Belfast._

Dated this _20th_ day of _March_ 19_53_

Andrew Lucas

Usual signature of applicant.

P.T.O.

E44186 Wt.43376-4180 24M(2) 3/52 Gp.58   F. & C. Ltd. London

more than four children. When Andrew and Mary took the keys and went for a for a look around, they were overwhelmed by the amount of space and the size of the rooms. There were four bedrooms, a separate living room, an inside bathroom and toilet, a kitchen with hot and cold taps, and a coal fire with coal-bunker out the back.

Although delighted with the new house and its size, both of them knew that a lot of work would have to be done in terms of painting and decorating, but it would be their home for the next 25 years. In addition to the house there was a front garden and at the back each family was allocated a 'plot' of land to cultivate and grow vegetables. The streets which were complete at that time were Wellhouse Crescent, Torran Road, Baldovan Crescent, Balado Road, Bartibeith Road and Ware Road.

Nearby was the Monklands Canal which would eventually be filled in to become part of the new M8 motorway, but in 1959 the waterway and the surrounding countryside provided a vast expanse of openness.

It would not be long before all the land would be consumed with houses, but there was no church, cinema or shops, so people had to travel back to Parkhead and Shettleston for supplies. Before long a feeling of isolation quickly set in, and in Andrew's case it was not a place he would come to like.

After digging and planting vegetables and flowers in the allocated plot of land behind the house, Andrew awoke one summer morning to find that all his plants and flowers had been vandalised. He was so disgusted that he never attempted to grow anything again. Nor did he make any great attempt to find work ashore, preferring the anonymity of the sea and the camaraderie of his fellow sailors.

As there was no church or shops when they moved to Easterhouse, 9 Balado Road – a three apaprtment house – became the substitute church until a new one could be built.

Increasingly Andrew was drawn back to Parkhead and his established drinking dens. His drinking spells became longer and sometimes his moods verged on the violent; his inability to cope with family life and the feeling of isolation in Easterhouse proving just too much for him at times.

As his children were growing up Andrew found it more and more difficult to cope with the demands of being a father, an absent one at that. And the tensions within the family were increasing as his children moved from schoolchildren into adolescence and adulthood.

Chapter 8

The Passing Away

The end of Andrew's life on earth came quietly and suddenly. Having been seriously ill for some time, Andrew was confined to bed. One day in February, 1980 at around 4am he became quite agitated and restless. Some time later he settled back in his bed, gave a deep sigh and closed his eyes. He was gone.

Death was a relief from the pain that he had been suffering. The accumulation of smoking up to 80 cigarettes a day – from Capstan Full Strength to Woodbine and Senior Service – finally took their toll. He did not say goodbye nor spoke any words; he just slipped quietly away to begin his new life. At his death he was surrounded by Mary, his wife of 38 years, their daughters, Anne and Agnes, and son, Thomas.

Andrew left behind a legacy of hard work and humour. He also left behind six children who each remember him in their own way. He was given the last rites of the Roman Catholic church and, after a Requiem Mass in St. John Ogilvy's RC Church, he was buried in Barrhead Cemetery.

No member of his family in the USA came over for the funeral. He was abandoned at birth by them and abandoned in death, but Andrew held no bitterness towards his family. He only ever wanted to be accepted by them. Despite reconciliation, Andrew never became close to them.

However Andrew did hold a bitterness and resentment towards the treatment that Merchant Seamen had been given during the Second World War. Despite being eligible for five war medals, Andrew refused to collect them. It appears that if you were a member of the Armed Forces, you were automatically 'given' your medal, however if you were attached to the Merchant Navy, a seaman had to 'apply' for his. Needless to say Andrew's medals have since been acquired by the family.

Andrew's contribution to the war effort, and that of his fellow Merchant Seamen, should not be underestimated. They were the unsung heroes of the war and it was their heroics and bravery that allowed Britain to survive the worst ravages of the conflict and ultimately ensure that victory was ensured.

Andrew loved his family and in his own way was proud of them all. He was particularly close to his grandson, Paul. Despite all that he suffered in his later years, Andrew still retained stoicism and a wicked sense of humour that only a life at sea can give.

For most of his working life – some 46 years – Andrew was at sea. He often remarked that he had sailed the world several times over in the course of his seafaring life. An extremely private man, he was reluctant to advance any notion of his heroism but was proud of the Merchant Navy and the men he had sailed with. In a world of 'instant' and false heroism, Andrew and many like him were testimony to a time when duty and obligation and sacrifice were the norm.

No-one should underestimate the bravery and sacrifice that seamen like Andrew and thousands of others gave so that Britain could survive WW2. Yet, like many working class men and women, there was no fanfare at his funeral, no eulogy, no heads of state, no recognition from HM Government; just a quiet, dignified service to commemorate a life well lived, a service to duty.

Andrew Lucas came into this world in 1919 and departed from it in 1980. He left no will, he had no estate. He did not own his own house. He served his country and looked after his family. He never revealed why he had been abandoned by his own mother and father. He left behind a mountain of memories and a handful of hope for a better life.

He navigated his way through the hardships of life with fortitude and determination. He survived all that life had to throw at him and still he kept on smiling and laughing. His life at sea shaped him into becoming the man that he was. His life was not an easy one, yet despite all of that he was a survivor. Many a lesser person would have crumbled under the weight of so many setbacks and trials.

Andrew, like so many of his compatriots, deserves to be remembered and saluted for all that he did for his country and his family. To paraphrase Winston Churchill 'never in the field of human conflict has so much been achieved by the men and women of the Merchant Navy'.

Exn. 2b.

Rotation Number
(for Office use only.)

Port of ~~NATIONAL SEA TRANS~~ ~~GLASGOW~~

APPLICATION TO BE EXAMINED
FOR A
CERTIFICATE OF EFFICIENCY AS LIFEBOATMAN.

Surname (in block letters) LUCAS   Other names ANDREW
No. of Discharge Book R189089   Rating A.B.
(which should accompany this application).
Date and Place of Birth 29.11.29
Permanent Address 20, Gleamhill St. Parkhead Hamilton
Description of Candidate   Height
(to be given where the applicant is not in possession   Colour of Eyes
of a Discharge Book).   Hair
                                              Complexion
                                              Tattoo or other Marks (if any)

I hereby apply to be examined for a Certificate of Efficiency as Lifeboatman.
Date 25.6.52   Signature of Candidate Andrew Lucas

The Seaman named above has applied to be examined for a Certificate of Efficiency
as Lifeboatman and a fee of One Shilling has been paid to me.
Dated at .... this .... day of 19
                                              (Signature of Superintendent).
To the Principal Officer,
  Ministry of Transport,
  Marine Surveyor's Office,   Mercantile Marine Office,

I have examined the Seaman named above for a Certificate of Efficiency as Lifeboatman
and he has Passed in the examination.
Dated this 27 day of June 19 52
                                              (Signature of Examiner).
To the Superintendent,   Name of vessel on
  Mercantile Marine Office,   which examined

(a)*
A Certificate of Efficiency No. 140914 has been issued to the above-named
Seaman this 27 day of June 1952, and his
discharge book has been endorsed accordingly.
(b)*
Applicant failed as stated above.
Dated this .... day of 19
                                              (Signature of Superintendent).

* Delete the
words that
do not apply.

(1) Principal Officer or the Surveyors,
     Ministry of Transport,
     Marine Surveyors' Office,
(2) The Registrar-General of Shipping and Seamen.

Note.—The application forms Exn. 2b. are to be forwarded monthly to the Registrar-General with
the Schedule 1 on which the fees have been brought to account.

(B4699) Wt. 41909—483 7,500 4/50 P. & N. Ltd. G813

Dis. A. No. R189089
Cert. of Compy. No. 8536
*Name of Master, Seaman   a Lucas
  or Apprentice
Birth: Date   Place
Rank or Rating   Sailor
Name and Official No. of Ship   Date of Engagement
                                    (Stamp of M.M.O.)
144223   15.5.51

*If Dis. A. is not produced, the surname should be in block capitals.
(92410C) Wt 14743/37 500,000 8/40 H, J, R & L, Ld Gp 684

"Laurentia"

SOCIAL & ATHLETIC CLUB.

○●○

Membership Card.

Season 1951.

D. MUNRO & SON, PRINTERS.

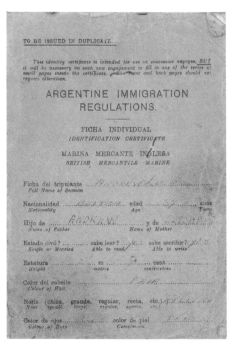

ARGENTINE IMMIGRATION REGULATIONS.

FICHA INDIVIDUAL
IDENTIFICATION CERTIFICATE

MARINA MERCANTE INGLESA
BRITISH MERCANTILE MARINE

Ficha del tripulante ....
Full Name of Seaman

Nacionalidad .... edad .... años
Nationality   Age   Years

Hijo de .... y de ....
Name of Father   Name of Mother

Estado civil? .... sabe leer? ...... sabe escribir? ......
Single or Married   Able to read   Able to write

Estatura .... m .... cent. ....
Height   metres   centimetres

Color del cabello ....
Colour of Hair.

Nariz (chica, grande, regular, recta, etc.)..........
Nose (small, large, regular, square, etc.)

Color de ojos.......... color de piel ....
Colour of Eyes   Complexion

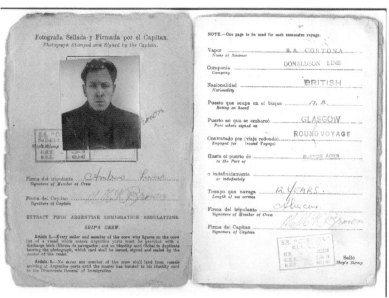

Fotografía Sellada y Firmada por el Capitan.
Photograph Stamped and Signed by the Captain.

Firma del tripulante ....
Signature of Member of Crew

Firma del Capitan ....
Signature of Captain

EXTRACT FROM ARGENTINE IMMIGRATION REGULATIONS.

SHIPS CREW.

Article 2.—Every sailor and member of the crew who figures on the crew list of a vessel which enters Argentine ports must be provided with a discharge book (libreta de navegación); and an identity card (ficha) in duplicate bearing the photograph, which card shall be issued, signed and sealed by the master of the vessel.

Article 3.—No master nor member of the crew shall land from vessels arriving at Argentine ports until the master has handed in his identity card in the Directorate General of Immigration.

NOTE.—One page to be used for each successive voyage.

Vapor .... S.S. CORTONA
Name of Steamer

Compania .... DONALDSON LINE
Company

Nacionalidad .... BRITISH
Nationality

Puesto que ocupa en el buque .... A. B.
Rating on board

Puerto en que se embarcó .... GLASGOW
Port where signed on

Contratado por (viaje redondo).......... ROUND VOYAGE
Engaged for (round Voyage)

Hasta el puerto de .... BUENOS AIRES
to the Port of

o indefinidamente ....
or indefinitely

Tiempo que navega .... 12 YEARS.
Length of sea service

Firma del tripulante ....
Signature of Member of Crew

Firma del Capitan ....
Signature of Captain

Sello
Ship's Stamp

ISSUED	EXPIRES	CITIZENSHIP	PLACE OF BIRTH
4-5-44		BRITISH	HAMILTON, SCOT.

AGE	HEIGHT	WEIGHT	COLOR EYES	COLOR HAIR	ALIEN REGISTRATION NO.
34	5'8	140	Blue	Brown	***** Alien Seaman

SOCIAL SECURITY NUMBER WU

None.

SERIAL No. 031 1466841

INDEX FINGER RIGHT HAND

Andrew Lucas
SIGNATURE

FORM NO. 6.

WESTERN UNION
(THE WESTERN UNION TELEGRAPH COMPANY)
(INCORPORATED IN THE STATE OF NEW YORK, U.S.A., WITH LIMITED LIABILITY.)

CABLEGRAM

ANGLO-AMERICAN TELEGRAPH CO., LD. CANADIAN NATIONAL TELEGRAPHS.

RECEIVED AT 8, WATERLOO STREET, GLASGOW, C. 2. (Tel. No. Central, 6363.)
Kirkintilloch, 1782. (After office hours)
Central Telex 2565.

82/17 CHICAGO ILL 53 16

1942 OCT 17 PM 6 08

NLT MR AND MRS ANDREW LUCAS

CARE B GALLAGHER 20 THORNHILLST PARKHEAD GLASGOW

DEAR ANDY AND MARY WISHING YOU BOTH BEST OF HAPPINESS

AND LUCK IN THE WORLD ON YOUR MARRIAGE MOTHER AND FAMILY

ARE HAPPY ABOUT IT MAY GOD BLESS YOU BOTH PLEASE WRITE TO

US

JOE AND NAN DOUGLAS 6241 SOUTHPARK +

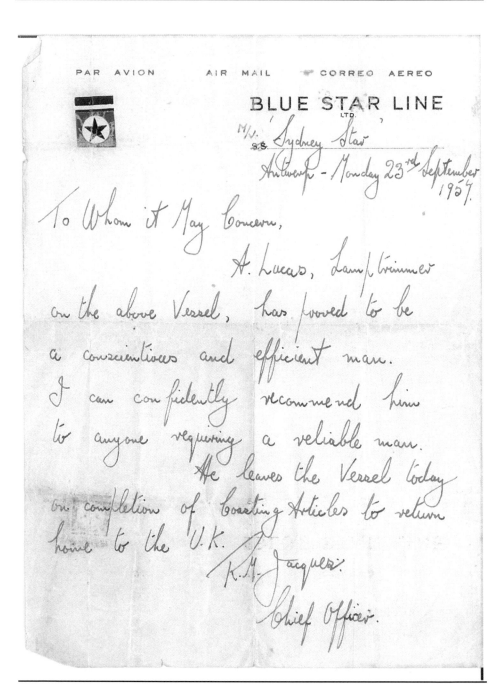

PAR AVION   AIR MAIL   CORREO AEREO

BLUE STAR LINE
LTD.

M/v.
s.s. Sydney Star

Antwerp - Monday 23rd September
1957.

To Whom it May Concern,

A. Lucas, Lamp trimmer
on the above Vessel, has proved to be
a conscientious and efficient man.
I can confidently recommend him
to anyone requiring a reliable man.
He leaves the Vessel today
on completion of Coasting Articles to return
home to the U.K.

K.M. Jacques.

Chief Officer.

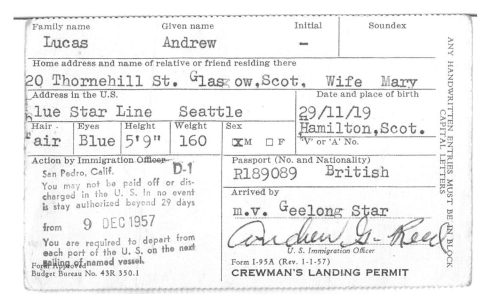

Family name	Given name		Initial	Soundex
Lucas	Andrew		–	

Home address and name of relative or friend residing there

20 Thornehill St. Glasgow,Scot, Wife Mary

Address in the U.S.					Date and place of birth
Blue Star Line Seattle					29/11/19
Hair	Eyes	Height	Weight	Sex	Hamilton,Scot.
Fair	Blue	5'9"	160	☒M ☐F	'V' or 'A' No.

Action by Immigration Officer	Passport (No. and Nationality)
San Pedro, Calif. **D-1**	R189089 British
You may not be paid off or discharged in the U. S. In no event is stay authorized beyond 29 days	Arrived by
	m.v. Geelong Star
from 9 DEC 1957	*[signature]*
You are required to depart from each port of the U. S. on the next sailing of named vessel.	U. S. Immigration Officer
Form Approved	Form I-95A (Rev. 1-1-57)
Budget Bureau No. 43R 350.1	**CREWMAN'S LANDING PERMIT**

ANY HANDWRITTEN ENTRIES MUST BE IN BLOCK CAPITAL LETTERS

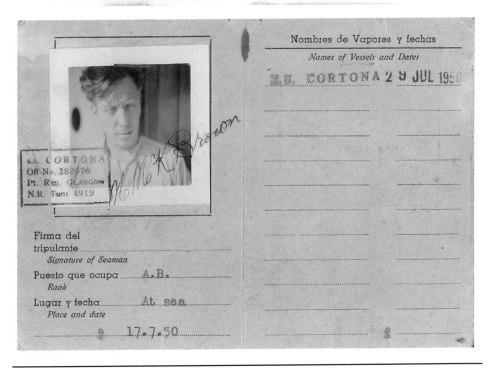

Nombres de Vapores y fechas

Names of Vessels and Dates

M.B. CORTONA 2 9 JUL 1950

s.s. CORTONA
Off No. 182076
Pt. Reg. GLASGOW
N.R. Tons 4919

Firma del
tripulante ....
   Signature of Seaman

Puesto que ocupa ...... A.B. ....
   Rank

Lugar y fecha ...... At sea ....
   Place and date
.... 17.7.50 ....

NAPOLI - VESUVIO

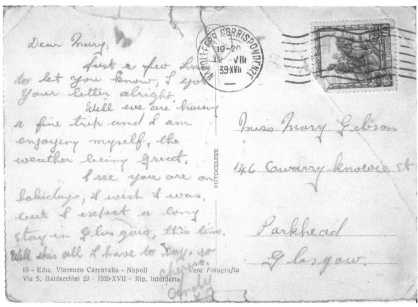

Dear Mary,

Just a few lines to let you know, I got your letter alright.

Well we are having a fine trip and I am enjoying myself, the weather being great.

I see you are on holidays, I wish I was, but I expect a long stay in Glasgow, this time. Well this is all I have to say, so

Miss Mary Gibson

146 Cavarry Knowie St

Parkhead

Glasgow

10 - Ediz. Vincenzo Carcavallo - Napoli   Vera Fotografia
Via S. Baldacchini 29 - 1939-XVII - Rip. interdetta

OCTOBER, 1, 1948

AT ST. THOMAS the Apostle church, Sept. 18, Marie Lucas, daughter of Andrew Lucas, became the bride of Xavier Savino. Celebrant of Nuptial Mass was Rev. Thomas P. Mulcahey. The Savinos will live on the South side.

1: Aunty Marie's Wedding

2: Uncle John, Aunty Marie & Elaine

3: Aunty Marie

4: Aunty Elaine

5: Dad & Friend

6: Aunty Marie & Elaine

7: Great Grandfather & Auntie ??

8: Uncle Thomas & Nan

9: Dad & Friend

10: Grandparents

11: Dad & Friends

12: Mum & Dad

13: Aunty Martha

14: Dad

15: Mum, Aunty Agnes & Sarah

16: Cousins

17: Grandfather

18: Aunties

19: Dad, Nan & Joe

20: Mum & Friend

21: Dad, Nan & Joe

22: Nieces

23: Sisters

24: Gibson & Lucas Family Gathering

25: Mum School Days

26: Dads Uncle

27: Dad & Friend

28: Gran & Family

29: Grandfather, Grandmother & Mary-Annie

30: Dad at Stork Club, New York

31: Wedding at St. Marks

33: Uncle John

32: Dad's & Family

34: Mum

35: Uncle John

36: Uncle Thomas & John

37: Mum & Dad

38: Grandfather, Grandmother & Uncle John

39: Uncle John & Aunty Marie

40: Dad's Football Team

41: Gibson Family

42: Uncle John & Aunty Marie & Elaine

43: Aunty Elaine & Marie

44: Mum & Kids

45: Dad & Friend

46: Mum & Dad at my Wedding

47: Aunty Marie

48: Mum & Friends

The Family History of Andrew Lucas

Andrew Lucas was an only surviving triplet, born on the 29 November 1919 at 5 Guthrie Street, Hamilton (*Hamilton, 647, entry no. 1322*). Their parents were Andrew Lucas, a coal miner and Elizabeth McCallion. He was born at 3.40 am.

His elder brother, James was born at 1.40 am and lived for 10 days (*Hamilton, 647, entry no. 509*) His younger brother, Charles was born 10 minutes after him, but only lived for 12 Days (*Hamilton, 647, entry no. 510*)

Andrew Lucas and Elizabeth McCallion

* Their marriage

> **District** – *Hamilton, County of Lanark, 647/oo, entry no. 233*
> **Date and Place** - *on the 22 October 1915 at 17 Almada Street, Hamilton, after Banns according to the Forms of the Established Church of Scotland*
> **Groom** – *Andrew Lucas, coal miner, bachelor, aged 23, residing at 17 Almada Street, Hamilton*
> **Bride** – *Elizabeth McCallion, spinster, aged 23, residing at 10 Guthrie Street, Hamilton*
> **Parents of Groom** – *John Lucas, late coal miner and Annie Lucas, m.s Jones*
> **Parents of Bride** – *Denis McCallion, tramway stableman and Annie McCallion, m.s Gallacher*
> **Celebrator** – *Douglas W Bruce, Minister of Cadzow Parish*
> **Witnesses** – *Frank Lucas and Mary Smith*
> **Registered** *on the 25 October at Hamilton*

John Lucas and Annie Jones

* **1901 census – Hamilton** (*647/00, Enumeration Book 20, pages 11 and 12*)

Allanshaw Rows

> *John Lucas, head, married, aged 49, coal miner, born Ireland*
> *Annie Lucas, wife, married, aged 45, born Ireland*
> *John Lucas, son, aged 24, coal miner, born Lanark, Wishaw*
> *Samuel Lucas, son, aged 21, coal miner, born Lanark, Wishaw*
> *Mary E Lucas, daughter, aged 17, born Lanark, Hamilton*
> *Robert Lucas, son, aged 14, shop boy, born Lanark, Hamilton*
> *Andrew Lucas, son, aged 9, scholar, born Lanark, Hamilton*
> *Francis Lucas, son, aged 6, scholar, born Lanark, Hamilton*

(AS can be seen below, the enumerator made a mistake in this entry. Francis was actually older than Andrew)

* **1891 census – Hamilton** (*647/00, Enumeration District 17, page 31*)

Allanshaw Rows

John Lucas, head, married, aged 38, coal miner, born Ireland
Annie Lucas, wife, married, aged 35, coal miner's wife, born Ireland
William J Lucas, son, aged 16, coal miner, born Wishaw, Lanarkshire
John Lucas, son, aged 14, coal miner, born Wishaw, Lanarkshire
Sam Lucas, son, aged 12, scholar, born Wishaw, Lanarkshire
Mary E Lucas, daughter, aged 7, scholar, born Hamilton, Lanarkshire
Robert Lucas, son, aged 4, born Hamilton, Lanarkshire
Thomas Lucas, son, aged 1, born Hamilton, Lanarkshire

*1881 census – Hamilton, (*647/00, Enumeration Book 17, page 59*)

Portland Place

John Lucas, head, married, aged 29, coal miner, born Ireland
Annie Lucas, wife, married, aged 27, born Ireland
William J Lucas, son, aged 6, scholar, born Lanarkshire, Wishaw
John Lucas, son, aged 4, born Lanarkshire, Wishaw
Samuel Lucas, son, aged 2, born Lanarkshire, Wishaw
John Jones, brother-in-law, unmarried, aged 25, coal miner, born Ireland
Mary Ann Lucas, sister, aged 13, scholar, born Ireland

Births of children (see photocopies of all their births)

(You will see that John Lucas had trouble remembering the date of his marriage. Also, he initially spelt his surname Lukes, then Luces and finally Lucas)

20 January 1875 at 3pm at 14 Steel Street, Wishaw – William James Lucas; parents married on the 1 January 1874 in the parish of Clones, County Monaghan, Ireland (*Cambusnethan, 628, entry no. 68*)

It therefore seems likely that John Lucas and Annie Jones came to Scotland sometime in 1874

Birth of John Lucas

District *– Cambusnethan, County of Lanark, 628/00, entry no. 994*
Name *– John Lukes*
Date and Place *– 14 December 1876 at 4 am at 14 Steel Street, Wishaw*
Parents *– John Lukes, coal miner and Annie Lukes, ms. Jones; married 31 December 1872, Clones, County Monaghan, Ireland*
Registered *by John Lukes on the 26 December at Wishaw*

5 April 1879 at 9 pm at 14 Steel Street, Wishaw – Samuel Lucas (*ibid, entry no. 242*)

Soon after this, the family appear to have moved to Hamilton where the rest of their children were born

7 June 1881 at 2 am at 150 Quarry Street, Hamilton – Alexander Lucas. This time, John Lucas gives the date of his marriage as 1 January 1872! (*Hamilton, 647, entry*

no. 531) Alexander died on the 24 December 1882 of whooping cough (*ibid, entry no. 533*)

30 March 1884 at 5 am at 171 Quarry Street, Hamilton – Mary Elenor Lucas. Again her father gives his year of marriage as 1872 (*ibid, entry no. 340*)

8 July 1886 at 3 am at McAlpine's Buildings, Beckford Street, Hamilton – Robert Lucas (*ibid, entry no. 746*)

1 January 1890 at 3 am at Allanshaw Rows, Hamilton – Thomas Lucas. This time his father gives the year of his marriage as 1873! (*ibid, entry no. 52*). Thomas died on the 23 October 1893 of croup (*ibid, entry no. 535*)

3 November 1894 at 1 am at the same place, Francis Lucas (*ibid, entry no. 1178*)

14 March 1898 at 1 pm at the same place – Andrew Lucas (*ibid, entry no. 341*)

* Death of John Lucas

> ***District*** *– Hamilton, 647/00, entry no. 94*
> ***Name*** *– John Lucas, married to Annie Jones*
> ***When and Where*** *– on the 5 March 1916 at 2.30 pm at 17 Almada Street, Hamilton*
> ***Age*** *- 60*
> ***Parents*** *– James Lucas, farm labourer and Helen Lucas, m.s McCallion (both deceased)*
> ***Cause of death*** *- Apoplexy*
> ***Registered*** *by John Lucas, son, 2 Park Terrace, Uddingston*

* Death of Annie Jones

> ***District*** *– Bothwell, 625/01, entry no. 84*
> ***Name*** *– Arabella Lucas, widow of John Lucas, coal miner (hewer)*
> ***When and Where*** *– on the 19 June 1941 at 5.5 pm at 24 Crofthead Street, Uddingston; usual residence 14 Victoria Street, Hamilton*
> ***Age*** *- 88*
> ***Parents*** *– James Jones, labourer (deceased) and Elizabeth Jones, m.s Hurkley? (deceased)*
> ***Cause of death*** *- Senility*
> ***Registered*** *by her son, John Lucas on the 30 June at Uddingston*

Birth of John Lucas

According to the IGI, there is a birth of a John Lucas to James and Ellen Lucas, Clones, County Monaghan on the 30 March 1849 (source given - the Parish Registers of Clones, 1682-1900) As John Lucas's parents were James Lucas and Ellen McCallion, it seems likely that this is his correct baptism. Monaghan is a parish in Northern Ireland.

Diane Baptie, October 2009

The Lucas family tree

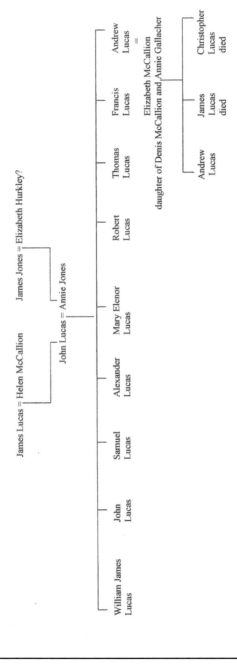

James Lucas = Helen McCallion   James Jones = Elizabeth Hurkley?

John Lucas = Annie Jones

| William James Lucas | John Lucas | Samuel Lucas | Alexander Lucas | Mary Elenor Lucas | Robert Lucas | Thomas Lucas | Francis Lucas | Andrew Lucas |

Andrew Lucas
=
Elizabeth McCallion
daughter of Denis McCallion and Annie Gallacher

| Andrew Lucas | James Lucas died | Christopher Lucas died |

Campaign Stars, Clasps and Medals instituted in recognition of Service in the War of 1939 -1945

NUMBER OF STARS, MEDALS, CLASPS OR EMBLEMS ENCLOSED	

Order in which the awards should be set up e.g.: for framing	DESCRIPTION OF RIBBON	Clasp or Emblem (if Awarded)
1. 1939-45 Star	Dark Blue, Red & Light Blue in three equal vertical stripes. This ribbon is worn with the dark blue stripe furthest from the left shoulder.	Battle of Britain
2. Atlantic Star	Blue, White & Sea Green shaded and watered. This ribbon is worn with the blue edge furthest from the left shoulder.	Air Crew of Europe or France & Germany
3. Air Crew Europe Star	Light Blue with black edges and in addition a narrow yellow stripe on either side.	Atlantic or France & Germany
4. Africa Star	Pale buff, with a central vertical red stripe & two narrower stripes, one dark blue & the other light blue. This ribbon is worn with the dark blue stripe furthest from the left shoulder.	8th Army or 1st Army or North Africa 1942-3
5. Pacific Star	Dark Green with red edges, a central yellow stripe, and two narrow stripes, one dark blue and the other light blue. This ribbon is worn with the dark blue stripe furthest from the left shoulder.	Burma
6. Burma Star	Dark Blue with a central red stripe and in addition two orange stripes.	Pacific
7. Italy Star	Five vertical stripes of equal width, one in red at either edge and one in green at the centre, the two intervening stripes being in white.	
8. France & Germany Star	Five vertical stripes of equal width, one in blue at either edge and one in red at the centre, the two intervening stripes being in white.	Atlantic
9. War Medal 1939-1945	A narrow central red stripe with narrow white stripe on either side. A broad red stripe at either edge, and two intervening stripes in blue.	Oak Leaf

Lucas's Surviving Family

Andrew Lucas
Derek Lucas
Raymond Lucas
Katrina Lucas
Rhonda Lucas
John Lucas
Thomas Lucas
Collette Lucas
Roisin Lucas
Mary Lucas
Ann Lucas
Paul Lucas
Oran Lucas
Agnes Lucas